ViP's

DIRECTORY OF

GIANT SCALE PLANS

VIP PUBLISHERS, INC.,

P.O. BOX 16103 COLORADO SPRINGS, COLORADO 80935

ISBN 0-934575-02-9

PRINTED IN THE USA

ACKNOWLEGEMENTS

It would have been impossible for us to put together this Directory of Large Plans without the co-operation and enthusiastic help of those people who supplied us with plans to evaluate. It goes without our saying it: all the plans designers represented by their work in the pages that follow have earned our gratitude for their generous co-operation. They have answered letters, supplied plans, and photographs, and in general, helped us to bring this guide to you.

Each plan is identified with the name of the supplier, and rather than list them again here, we'll ask that you appreciate their generosity as you use this guide. Without exception, they are good friends and generous people. The work they have put into producing plans for our use often goes without real reward other than the satisfaction of knowing there are many of their 'brain children' out there, boring holes in the sky and bringing pleasure to other model builders.

Anyone who has ever designed a plan and built from it knows the many hours of painstaking work which go into such a project. Without the designers, modeling would not be the fun nor the challenge it is. Our very sincere thanks to them all, and to those of you who are now in the process of working on plans (which we'll be happy to add to future Volumes of this Directory).

Col. John A. de Vries
Colorado Springs, Colorado
USA

Dick Phillips
Sidney, British Columbia
Canada

TABLE OF CONTENTS

WORLD WAR I

BETWEEN THE WARS, MILITARY & CIVILIAN A/C

"GOLDEN AGE" RACING AIRPLANES

WORLD WAR II "WARBIRDS"

POST-WAR CIVILIAN A/C & HOMEBUILTS

NON-SCALE "GIANTS" & OTHERS

Cover: Wendell Hostetler's magnificent quarter-scale model of Roscoe Turner's Wedell-Williams Racer, in "GILMORE" trim. Hostetler photo. Full scale photos courtesy Bob Banka's Scale Model Research. Others courtesy the designers.

INTRODUCTION

We have felt for some time that a directory to the large scale plans available would be a valuable guide to those who build from plans. However, a directory would be a simple listing of the plans which are available on the open market and would not tell a builder much about them. Thus, this volume. What we have tried to do is offer some guidance, from a position of experience, to the value of plans currently available.

Keep in mind that "currently available" is not graven in stone. What is available now may not always be so. The plans we have included are ones which have been made available in quantity and therefore many copies are in existence. Even if a plan is found to be no longer available from the original supplier, there are copies in someone's collection. These may be hard to find (and "borrow") but they are out there somewhere.

Building from someone else's plan is not true "scratch building". It is, by definition, constructing a model designed and drawn by the builder himself. Building from a plan done by another is actually "plans building". It should not be considered scratch building, although it is frequently referred to by that term.

There are several advantages to plans building. There are many plans for scale airplanes which do not exist as kits. They provide a "new" subject which may not be common on the contest circuit. The cost of large kits is also a consideration. A model, built from a plan may cost a good deal less money than a similar model built from a kit. In building from a plan, alterations may be made to duplicate a particular airplane more easily than such changes might be made in a kit. The builder's favorite methods of construction are more easily accommodated when a plan is used rather than a kit. Material substitutions can be made without "wasting" any kit materials.

There are some drawbacks to plans building, of course. All the parts must be made, which takes time and requires some additional shop equipment for ease of such manufacture. In effect, the builder creates a "kit" from which to build the model. This requires that the modeler transfer patterns to the material being used and the ability to fabricate parts accurately. Tools which make this work much easier are a bandsaw and a sanding disk. Such tools make any construction project easier, of course, and their addition to your collection of shop tools will valuable for all most of your model-building projects, not just for plans building.

Some of the accessories required to construct a "plans-built" model may not be readily available. Happily,there are many manufacturers providing items today that aren't easily made by the builder. Items such as cowls, wheel pants, landing gear wires or blanks and cabane struts are becoming more readily available from accessory manufacturing firms. These items are usually good quality and save considerable time over making them yourself.

Our comments on the suitability of plans will necessarily be subjective; each of us is affected by his own experience and preferences and the authors are no exception. Both of us have a good deal of experience in the hobby and each of us has built many hundreds of models from kits and plans as well as our own drawings. The suggestions and recommendations we make in the following pages are the distillation of that experience and we hope you will find the information of value when it comes to making a decision as to whether or not to build from a particular plan.

We have contacted as many of the plans suppliers as we could locate. Most have agreed to cooperate with us in supplying copies of their plans and photos of a model built from the plan. In a few cases no photo was available and a sketch or partial three-view has been used. Photos were preferred, of course, and we have used them where available.

Our "library" of plans now tops the 250 mark! Including all of them in a single volume would be a practical impossibilty. Thus, our Directory of Large Plans will be published in four or five books. Subsequent volumes will include evaluations of completely different sets of model drawings. We will use succeeding books in this series to update those volumes that have "gone before".

Anyone producing a plan is invited to forward a copy, along with a photo of a completed model (5 X 7 black and white is preferred) to be considered for future volumes.

Our format will consist of a photo of a model built from the plan in question, a brief record of the specifications of the model and a capsule comment on the plan. This is for your quick review, so you can winnow out those plans which do not suit your purposes. Then follows a brief history of the original aircraft (if a scale model) along with sources of documentation on the prototype. Lastly, we'll critique the plan in some detail, outlining the degree of difficulty represented in building the model, any special skills needed, availability of accessory parts (i.e. Cowl, wheel pants, cabane struts, landing gear etc.) and other pertinent information.

Obviously, we have not been able to build a model from every plan we have covered here. Such a task would be a life's work and leave little time for anything else! However, calling on our experience with plans building, we have tried to give a reliable judgement of the suitability and skill required in order to create a flyable model from the plans covered here. In many cases we have relied on the plans supplier as to the flying characteristics of a model built from his plan. There is liable to be a degree of subjectivity in such comments!

We hope you will find the information contained in this Directory of value in making your decision as to which model to build from plans. Hopefully, we'll introduce you to a set of plans which you didn't know existed.

GOOD BUILDING --

GOOD FLYING --

SOFT LANDINGS!

BUILDING FROM PLANS

Building a model airplane from a plan is not much different than doing so from a kit. The actual construction procedures and sequences are no different. The difference between them lies in the amount of preparation required to build from plans.

In effect, it is necessary to make up a kit, then build it. Some modelers prefer to make the parts required as the need for them arises during construction. Some prefer to make the parts needed before starting assembly. Whichever method is chosen is up to the individual modeler. There are good and bad points about either method.

The builder who makes up his parts as he goes along can begin construction almost immediately. There's no long period of parts making required before getting started, and this appeals to the impatient among us. The difficulty with having to stop from time to time to make up the next items needed is, that it is possible to 'lose one's place' and forget some important detail which may require some back-tracking later.

On the other side of the coin, the builders who make all the parts up first can then proceed as with a kit, going from one detail to the next in an orderly way and not getting confused if they leave construction for a time.

The difficulty is much lessened if there is a building manual with the plan set. This set of directions may be checked off as each item is completed and there's little danger that the builder will forget some important detail.

PATTERNS

The first order of business in plans building is the need to make patterns for the parts required. This can take many forms, and the most important thing to remember is the need for accuracy. Parts which do not match the plan sheets will not be very likely to fit the model properly either.

NOTE: Due to the possibility of plans changing shape with changes in humidity, or through the means used to reproduce them, some parts patterned EXACTLY from the plan sheets may still not fit properly into place. Some trimming or sanding will be required in even the best drawn plans.

Those parts which are square and which do not have odd shapes are easily measured out and drawn onto the building material. There is not much need to prepare an elaborate pattern to transfer them to the building material if this can readily be done with a ruler and pencil. Just be careful that corners intended to be square, are, and the rest will take care of itself.

For any other parts, the simplest method of making patterns for them is to cut the plan patterns out, glue them in place on the building material and cut around the patterns.

If this method is to be used, do not use a water based adhesive to glue the pattern to the material. Water-based glues may cause the paper to shrink and/or change shape, defeating the purpose of having a pattern at all. In addition, the pattern must always be removed from the material before assembly. Paper between parts glued together can produce a very weak joint which will come apart at some future (and often inopportune) moment.

Rubber cement fills the requirement quite well in that it is unlikely to be the cause of any deformation of the pattern and it permits fairly easy removal of the pattern (and the rubber cement) after the parts have been cut.

Many prefer not to cut the plan up in order to make the patterns, and so must find some other way of transferring patterns to the building material.

Photo-copying of the patterns is a method often used to make up patterns which do not destroy the plan sheets. Care must be taken here to assure the copier used makes accurately-sized copies. Many do not and it may be necessary to search out a commercial copy firm that has a machine which will produce accurate patterns. Once the correct patterns have been made by this method, it is an easy matter to transfer them to the material being used, providing the building material will tolerate some heat.

Most modern copiers use a plastic powder to produce the copy. This plastic is fused to the face of the paper by application of heat which melts the plastic onto the paper. If this copied pattern is placed face down onto the construction material and heat is applied to the back of the copy, enough of the fused plastic will be transfered to the building material to reproduce exactly what is on the paper pattern. This is a simple, quick, and effective transfer and no expensive equipment is required. A household electric iron works quite well.

Failing all of the above, the patterns may be traced onto any transparent material, then cut out and traced onto the building material. A number of clear or colored thin film plastics are available for such a purpose. The writer has access to unexposed, developed, X-Ray film which is an ideal pattern material. The emulsion side takes pencil lines very well, and it is thick enough to trace easily when it comes time to transfer the patterns to the building material. There is now a plastic sheet on the hobby market which is intended for this purpose and it works very well in transferring shapes to our building material.

PARTS MAKING

Once the patterns have been applied to the building material, it is a relatively simple process to cut them out in preparation for assembly. The ubiquitous Dremel reciprocating saw does a fine job of this work and the balsa parts are a breeze to cut. Plywood is not a great deal harder to cut than balsa, but takes a little longer.

An even handier tool is a bandsaw. As the blade cuts continuously in only one direction, the cut is easier to control and binding of the blade is a lot less likely. Black & Decker make a medium sized, electric drill driven bandsaw which is quite reasonably priced (less than $100). A variety of saw blades are available for this fine tool, including metal cutting blades, and it is a useful addition to the shop of anyone who intends to do any amount of building from plans.

A sanding disk with a good solidly mounted table at right angles to the disk is also a very handy tool, and permits rapid sanding to final shape of all manner of parts and materials. Using an appropriate type of disk allows for very precise sanding of wood or plastic parts to almost any shape. The use of a metal abrasive disk will permit accurate shaping of aluminium or other light gauge metal parts as well. While not used as often as a disk sander, a motorized drum sander is also a handy tool for parts making.

WIRE BENDING

One other tool needed in building from plans is a sturdy wire bender which will be needed to bend the many landing gear and cabane wires required. Many of the plans included in these directories call for quarter inch piano wire, bent to complex shapes. Doing so is made a great deal easier with a tough bender able to do the job.

The alternative is to heat the wire red hot, bend it to the required shape and then re-temper it. This is most easily done by placing the wire in an oven, raising the temperature to 350 degrees, maintaining it there for an hour or more and then shutting off the heat. The wire is not removed at this time. The oven is allowed to cool gradually until the wire can be removed safely with the bare hand. It will then be roughly at the same temper as was the case before heat was used to shape it. While this method works well, it is a hassle to provide adequate heat with a propane torch to get the wire red hot to start with, let alone the possible hazards involved. A good sturdy bender is a better solution.

MATERIALS

The stick wood used in construction of many of the plans shown in these directories is occasionally referred to as hardwood. While spruce, pine, fir and other such woods are a good deal harder than balsa, they are more properly referred to as 'softwoods'. True hardwoods are such as Oak, Walnut and the like.

For our use in plans building, any straight-grained, clear softwood is adequate. One of the best is Sitka Spruce which is what we usually buy when we get our spruce sticks from the hobby shop. Such woods as Pattern pine, basswood and fir may also be used. Many modelers cut their own material from boards of these softwoods. Cutting one's own material is both economical and convenient as the board stock is often easily obtainable and the sizes required may be cut to suit the plan being built from. The lengths needed are often greater than are available 'ready-cut' so making one's own material has a number of advantages over buying it pre-cut.

Once the parts have been fabricated, and the stick material provided, whether all at once or piecemeal, construction can begin. If all the parts have been made before construction is started, the job of assembling the model is no different than building from a kit. The major difference is that many more subjects are available than if kits were the modeler's only source. There'll be a considerable saving over the cost of most large kits, too.

1/4 SCALE

FOKKER EINDECKER (E.III)

FROM: John Lockwood, 1696 Griffith, Clovis, Ca. 93612

SPAN: 99 1/2"   CHORD: 15 5/16"   DOD: 4   AREA: 1393 Sq. In.

LENGTH: 71 1/2"   WEIGHT: 11-12#   ENGINE: .91

HISTORICAL:

The Fokker E-Series of monoplanes represent Anthony Fokker's first true warplanes -- fighters equipped with synchronized machine guns. They owed their basic configuration to a Morane sport plane that Fokker acquired for 500 marks in January, 1914. Ever enterprising, the Dutch builder modified the French design to a welded steel tube fuselage and dubbed it the M5 -- as a civilian aircraft. He used 50 hp Gnome rotary engines to power his production aircraft until German Oberursel rotaries of greater horsepower were in production. Like other warplanes, the Fokker E's (for Eindecker -- single winged or monoplane) were successively modified to improve performance. When Anthony got to the E.III version, power had been doubled (to 100 hp) and the craft was capable of carrying two machine guns! A special model was built for Max Immelman that carried three machine guns, but the little monoplane was substantially overextended with such an overload. The E.III (Fokker designation: M14) was responsible for the so-called 1915 "Fokker Scourge" and gave the German air service an almost insurmountable advantage over Allied aircraft of the same period. Although limited in availability and assigned to only the best German airmen, the E.III only had to be "pointed" at an enemy aircraft and another victory was almost assured.

The E.III Fokker was powered by the 100 hp Oberursel rotary that gave a top speed of 87 mph. The wing span was 31'3" and the bird was 23' 7" long and weighed 1475 lbs. fully loaded. Enough fuel was carried for 1 1/2 hours of flight and the service ceiling was less than 10,000 ft. Aileron control was through the use of wing warping and there were no fixed tail surfaces. The landing gear array was wonderously complex and an identification feature of this early WW I fighter. Immelman and Boelke, noted early German aces, flew the Eindecker to achieve their reputations.

PLAN:

While not the slick and very neat looking plan of the professional plans supplier, Lockwood's Eindecker is a plan which can intrigue you even if you are not a WWI buff. If you are, you'll be hooked as soon as the plan is unrolled! The prototype model won Grand Champion at Morgan Hill's WWI Scale Jamboree in 1979. Considering that it uses wing warping as did the original full scale airplane, it's no real wonder!

The structure appears to be almost too light when the plan is first viewed. However a careful review leads us to believe it's quite capable of carrying the loads which will likely be placed on it.

Some of the structure is deceptively simple. The fuselage sides, for example, are simple structures and could be put together in a relatively short time. However, once the finer points are begun, there can be complications. Be prepared for some exacting work as progress is made in construction. The fuselage sides are made from 3/32 inch balsa sheeting, reinforced with 1/8 X 1/4 strip stock. The lightening holes in the sides are optional and were not on the prototype. The fuselage is slab-sided and is square in all directions except for the curved top of the forward fuselage area.

The landing gear is a wire bender's and a plumber's delight as there is so much of it. Between wire and brass tubing, there are literally dozens of parts to be made up and assembled, mainly by soldering. There are a good many small metal parts to be made up in order to complete the EIII. Some of them are quite small and their size and shape are somewhat critical. Care must be taken in preparing and assembling these parts or the effect of them will be lost. If they are not to be done right, better not to have started the project.

The rudder and elevator (there is no fin or stabilizer) are parts which will require care in building. The stab is " full flying" and must be built strongly, as it is supported by only one main structural member. The same is true of the rudder, and, here again, many small parts are required so the two tail group members will operate as intended. The rudder is basically 3/32 inch sheet with ribs attached on both sides. The outer edge is laminated from two pieces of 3/32 X 1/4 balsa strip stock which isn't a problem as you'll already have the rudder as a pattern to form them around. The "stabilator" is heavily gusseted and requires it. Take care in building here as the strength is necessary to withstand the loads it will be subjected to.

The wing will challenge the builder's skill. The airfoil is under-cambered and quite thin, requiring some skill to prepare the 28 ribs necessary. (Not to mention the skill necessary to cover an under-cambered wing!) The structure itself is actually quite simple, it's getting it all together that will be the fun part. The wing uses wing warping instead of ailerons -- and it works. The designer suggests that wing warping works better with a little co-ordinated rudder from time to time. (This has been one of the authors' experience with a similar model. The wing warping causes a bank to be initiated slowly and it is difficult to recover without the use of the rudder.)

DEGREE OF DIFFICULTY:

As mentioned above, a wire-bender's delight and a plumber's nightmare, the Eindecker is championship class (as has already been proven). Built with the care and attention it deserves, the model could be a real contender in a scale contest. Our '4' rating indicates it doesn't just fall into place. Be prepared for some delicate and exacting work.

1/4 SCALE

FOKKER D-VII

FROM: Behren's Plan Service, 31-27 Healey Ave, Far Rockaway, N.Y. 11691

SPAN: 88" (U) 72 3/4" (L) CHORD: 15 3/4" - 12" DOD:3 AREA: 2160 Sq. In.

LENGTH: 70 3/4" WEIGHT: Unspecified ENGINE: Quadra 35

HISTORICAL:

To try to write a "blurb", giving the history of the Fokker D-VII (D-7), is a difficult task. It's been done by many authors whose works have gained wide distribution ever since World War I. Literally, hundreds of model drawings of the D-VII have been made for everything from solid "shelf models" to Giant Scale. Thus, we'll use this part of or D-7 write-up to serve as a sort of "super documentation" for Germany's number one fighter of the Great War.

Joe Nieto's Smithsonian drawings of the D-VII are, arguably, the best ones available. Appearing first in the August and September 1951 issues of Model Airplane News, they were reprinted in the August, 1957 issue of the same magazine. They are available as 3/4"=1 ft. blueprints from the National Air and Space Museum's plans service and appear in MAN's Scale Book #1.

From the color and markings viewpoint, the better sources of information are to be found in the U.S.

versions of the Cross & Cockade quarterly Journals. Too many references to be included here, C&C articles described the standard hexagonal camouflage system as well as the outlandish paint schemes indulged in by the German Flying Circuses and their Aces. Although C&C U.S. is now defunct, copies of old Journals **are available** from: Harry Miller, Box U, Norwalk, CA, 90651.

The Fokker D-VII specs. are impressive. Upper wing span was 29' 3"; length was 22' 10" and it was 9' high. Powered by either a 160 or 180 hp Mercedes in-line "6", the D-VII topped 117 mph and had a service ceiling of 16,400 ft. It was built by Fokker and his arch-rival, Albatros. It "lived" into the 30's, as a front-line fighter for several nations' air forces.

PLAN:

This Behren's plan is rather plain, but clear and easy to read. Three plan sheets and a construction and 'pilots' manual complete the set.

The fuselage is made up from 1/4 square spruce stick material, gussetted at the joints. Only main longerons are called out as spruce, and changing the remainder of the material to spruce will produce considerably greater strength with a minimal weight increase. Construction is quite simple and should create no problems.

The firewall is shown as 1/4 inch plywood. The authors prefer a stronger material than this and going to half-inch material is recommended.

Cabane struts and landing gear wires are shown full sized on the plan. the cabane struts show a loop at the top and this shape will require some care in bending. The loops are small enough to pass a bolt but restrict passage of the head. It would be well to attempt this end of the cabanes first, before cutting the wire to length!

Tail group members are framed over the plan using stick material. Curved outer edges are laminated from thin strip stock and the straight edges are stick stock. These are all quite simple and easy to construct.

Box spars are used in the wings and these will produce wings of considerable strength. The vertical sides of the box are 1/16 inch plywood separated by 1/8 by 1/4 inch spruce sticks. This type of spar was common in full scale airplane production and has great strength in relation to it's weight. These are not hard to fabricate, but care should be taken to assure that all glue joints are well made. The wing ribs are slipped over these spars in order to assemble the wing.

Ailerons are present only in the upper wing and the servo installation shown places the servos in the wing near the ailerons. This will require the use of quite long servo leads in order to reach the receiver. Test the radio to be sure it will not be affected by interference from these long leads, or use Ace Noise Traps or similar equipment to eliminate the potential problem.

The scale airfoil is under-cambered and will require some care when covering to assure the covering material attaches securely to the undersurface of the wing. (A sport airfoil is shown on the plan which is semi-symmetrical. This may provide better flying characteristics than the scale airfoil and will certainly be easier to cover.)

The upper wing is shown as one-piece, and the lower wings attach to the fuselage sides. The method of attachment is not made clear on the plan sheets, but spar pockets are built into the lower part of the fuselage to support the lower wing. The 'N' struts will need to be well anchored in order to assure the proper location (and permanence) of the lower wing.

A fiberglass cowl is available from Fiberglass Master for the DVII. Ordering details are in the construction manual along with an order form. The sides of the forward fuselage are covered with a sheet of very light plywood in order to duplicate the metal sides of the forward fuselage in the original airplane. Making up these two sides will tax the ingenuity of most model builders.

DEGREE OF DIFFICULTY:

There is little here to make any great difficulty for the experienced. A flyable and attractive model can be produced from this plan with comparative ease. The newcomer would be well advised to start with something a little easier, or have some experienced help available. Thus, our rating of '3' for this plan.

30% FULL-SIZE

FOKKER D-VIII

FROM: Jim Messer Model Products, 106 Valleyview Dr., Allegany, N.Y. 14706

SPAN: 100" CHORD: 12 1/4 - 18 1/4 DOD: 4 AREA: 1225 Sq. In.

LENGTH: 66 7/8" WEIGHT: Unspecified ENGINE: Quadra 35

HISTORICAL:

The Fokker D-VIII (D.8) was dubbed the 'Flying Razor' by Allied aircrew who encountered it in combat. A parasol monoplane, it was reputed to be difficult to see when approaching head-on.

Although the designation D-VIII is the one we modelers use, the principal production version of the aircraft was officially designated the E.V (Eindecker No. 5). The D.8 was almost a 'throw-back' when it appeared. After providing the magnificent Fokker D-VII, with it's stationary Mercedes engine, a rotary powered high winged monoplane is hard to explain. It performed reasonably well and was very maneuverable albeit not very fast. It wasn't that much of an improvement over it's predecessor. Apparently Fokker had a stock of readily available rotaries and had experienced some difficulty acquiring the Mercedes engines -- hence the DVIII. Engines used were the 110 HP Oberursel UR.11 in the E.V. versions and the 145 HP Oberursel UR.111 in the later D-VIII versions.

The D.8 has long been a favorite of model builders since the 'real airplane' featured a plywood covered wing. (1.5 mm in thickness) It's easy to duplicate and looks rather 'modern' plus it provides good strength. In it's full scale form, it proved to be scandal to Anthony Fokker. Wing failures of early E.V.'s, due to sloppy construction practices in the first 139 built, almost did the Fokker Company in as far as the German Army flying service was concerned.

Span was 27' 7". length 19' 4". Absolute ceiling was 22,000 feet and it took approximately 36 minutes to get there -- a rather rapid climb rate for a WWI fighter.

PLAN:

This Fokker D-VIII was designed and drawn by the S.T.A.R.S. of Olean, N.Y. This group has been in the forefront of the move to larger models for some years and is well known for their abilities. This Fokker D-VIII was designed in 1979 and shows the group's capabilities even then.

At approximately 1/3 scale, this is a large model. The three plan sheets (no manual) are quite complete although some past experience with plans building will be required in order to complete this project. This plan requires a good deal of study in order to determine what is required, so experience and the ability to read plans will be an absolute necessity.

In order to build the model as it is shown on the plan, some shaped strip stock will be required. The main fuselage longerons are 'L' shaped and, as this work is usually done with a router, it will be necessary to have the use of one and be able to produce the lengths of longeron needed. However, in the interests of simplicity, square stock could be used so long as proper allowances are made in the other parts involved. This will require some time and considerable care, and it may be easier to make them up as indicated. Basswood is specified and it will certainly accept such shaping as well as almost any other wood.

Considerable wire bending is required as there are ten different wires required for the cabane struts and landing gear.

The empennage is conventional construction; only the rudder requires it's outer edge to be laminated from strip stock. The stabilizer is huge and will provide good stability despite the rather short-coupled fuselage.

A number of small metal fitting of relatively complicated shapes will need to be made, so some skill in metal working is required to complete this project.

The wing is also quite large and, as it is tapered, will require the patterning and making of a large number of wing ribs. There are 28 in total, two of each required, plus 8 more of the largest rib. As these ribs are also cap-stripped, a good deal of time will be spent building the wing.

The wing is shown as one piece, which makes for a large assembly to be transported. At almost nine feet long, it takes up some room!

Controls are shown as being cable operated (both directions, of course) so some experience with rigging such a control system will be required. (Or gained during construction !) This method of transferring movement from a servo to a control surface requires cable with NO STRETCH and considerable care in assembly. The aileron control runs are inside the wing, naturally, so they will not be accessible after covering. They had better be right the first time!

Controls to the elevator are partly inside the fuselage so will require care in assembly in order to avoid any problems. Both sides of the elevator are rigged this way, so it will be a challenge to anyone but the experienced in this method of control. Although it is not made clear on the plan, the rudder should be cable controlled as well. Some ingenuity will be needed to arrange this control run.

The small winglet between the wheels is cut from foam and sheeted, so is easy to make up. A sketch is included showing how to make this and assemble it in place.

The Fokker D-VIII at this size makes a most impressive model on the ground and in the air. It will attract considerable attention wherever it is shown.

DEGREE OF DIFFICULTY:

This is no project for any but the well experienced builder. There is much work to be done, both in preparation for building and during the building process itself. Some parts needed will require considerable care and skill. Our rating of '4' leans toward a '5'. Be prepared for lots of painstaking work.

1/4 SCALE

FOKKER DR.1 TRIPLANE

FROM: M.C. Beaulieu's Plans Service, 84 University St., Presque Isle, ME.

SPAN: 66.5" (U) 56.25" (M) 61.5" (L) DOD: 3 LENGTH: 55" WEIGHT: UNKNOWN

CHORD: 12" (U) 9.5" (M) 10" (L) AREA: 1815 Sq.In. ENGINE:Q35

HISTORICAL:

Everlastingly associated with "the Red Baron", many modelers are surprised to learn that only about 350 Fokker Dr.I triplanes were built during WW I. Relatively unstable in model form, the "Tripe" has really come into its own as an R/C subject.

Although there were several three-wingers developed during the Great War, Anthony Fokker's "inspiration" for a triplane fighter came to him through the auspices of the British.

A captured Sopwith Tripe served as the example. The aerodynamic idea of an airplane with three wings stacked above one another was to create a craft with superb manueverability -- a fact that was achieved by the Dr.I. Of course, all of those airfoils created a fantastic amount of drag so the compromise resulted in a bird that was s-l-o-w, even more so with only 110 horsepower available! And, a light, small tripe, with a narrow gear tread, was a "bear" on the ground, particularly when a rotary engine is spinning all of its cylinders up front.

From the modelling viewpoint, Joe Nieto's three-views (from MAN's book of WW I drawings or the 3/4"=1ft. blueprints from the National Air and Space Museum) are the accepted documentation.

There are a host of color and markings references, the best of which are to be found in old C&C Journals (see the Fokker D.VII write-up for C&C sources).

For scaling purposes, the Fokker Dr.I's upper wing spanned 23'7" and the tiny tripe was only 18'11" long. Top speed was 103 mph at 13,000 feet and the bird had a service ceiling of 19,580 ft. Max. Gross Weight was only 1,290 lbs and the Dr.I's 19 gallon fuel tank could keep it airborne for two hours.

PLAN:

Mike Beaulieu's plans are perhaps not as well known as some, but they are excellent quality, well drawn and clear. While there is not a lot of detail on the plan sheets, they are certainly adequate to the needs of the experienced builder. Although not for the beginner, the Fokker DR.1 or Triplane is not a particularly difficult project.

Two of the materials called out in the plan; Lauan Plywood and Basswood may be substituted for if not available in your location. Sig's Lite Ply and Spruce in the same sizes would be quite adequate.

The fuselage is quite conventional stick construction done over the plan. Only a few formers are required so pattern and part making is at a minimum. Plywood gussets are shown at all fuselage joints, a practice which the authors highly recommend. The fuselage is also shown internally braced with wire or thread. This bracing may have some structural function, but is probably not required for flight. A cabane strut assembly is available from Biz Cap. A glass cowl is available from T & D Fiberglass Specialties. (See SOURCE section for addresses.)

Tail feathers are also conventional construction with the exception of the elevator leading edge and the rudder hinge spar both of which are made from 3/8" arrow shaft. The outline of the all-flying rudder is made from laminations of 1/16" bass. Balsa would do quite nicely for this area if bass is not available. (Spruce at 1/16" might not take kindly to the fairly tight curves required. Soaking the spruce in water with a little household ammonia in it and careful handling would also do the trick.) The elevator and rudder are shown as cable operated although not in detail. Some ingenuity will be required to set this type of control in place and get it operating properly. It is an excellent method of control, but must be carefully engineered and constructed. If desired, conventional pushrods could be used.

Wings are also quite normal model structure except for the number of panels required. Only the upper wing has ailerons and these are shown cable operated. Leading edge of the ailerons is also 3/8" arrow shaft. As the airfoil on all wings is under-cambered, some care must be taken to assure the wings are built true. All panels are shown on the plan. Covering under-cambered wings can be a chore if it has not been attempted before. Several good methods exist for covering such wings and some research (or help) may be required.

Wing incidence is shown as + 2 degrees (Upper) and + 1.5 degrees on the mid and low wings. This may require some adjustment as, ideally, the upper wing should stall last.

Due to the cable operated control surfaces, a number of small metal parts must be made and a quantity of C.B. pulley assemblies is required. Some Proctor pulleys and turnbuckles are also necessary and these parts can be expensive. Numerous metal parts are also required in the cabane and interplane strut structures. The cable for control surface movement must be chosen carefully. It should not stretch. MacWhite aircraft grade (3/64") cable is specified; a plastic covered light steel cable (fishing leader) could be substituted. Be sure the RX antenna is routed well clear of such cables.

DEGREE OF DIFFICULTY:

While not for the rank beginner, this DR.1 Triplane should not give the experienced any great difficulty. It should also be a stable and good flying model. Our rating of 3 indicates it is about in the middle as far as difficulty of construction is concerned.

1/4 SCALE (22%)

FOKKER DR-1 TRIPLANE

FROM: Nick Ziroli, 29 Edgar Drive, Smithtown, N.Y. 11787

SPAN: 63" CHORD: 12 - 10 1/2 - 10 1/2 AREA: 1560 Sq. In.

LENGTH: 52" WEIGHT: 12 - 15# DOD: 3 ENGINE: Quadra 35

HISTORICAL:

Made famous (or notorious) depending on which side you were on, by Baron von Richthofen, the Fokker Triplane was distinguished by the wild color schemes devised by its pilots and its impressive 'kill' record during the 1914-1918 War to End All Wars.

Relatively small with a span of 23 feet, 7 inches, the DR-1 carried a brace of Spandau 7.92 mm machine guns firing through the propeller arc, using an interrupter gear, which sometimes worked and sometimes didn't, much to the dismay of the 'de-propped' pilot.

PLAN:

Another from Ziroli showing his usual clear and concise technique. The plan set consists of three sheets, no building manual, but none should be necessary. Numerous construction notes on the plan sheets will lead almost anyone through the construction process. The structure is simple, very strong and flies well on the small Quadra. It won the combat event at Old Rheinbeck in 1981. Ziroli recommends against the use of a larger engine as unnecessary.

The fuselage sides are made from 1/8 inch poplar plywood (Sig's Lite-Ply) and require a little work to lay out the pattern and then to cut. Several lightening holes are shown and should be cut out as indicated.

A number of cut parts are required, but the number is not that great, so the pattern making and cutting the parts will not be an arduous task.

Fuselage construction will proceed quickly, once all the parts are cut and should take no more than an evening's work using one of the C/A glues to have it substantially framed up.

Stabilizer and elevator construction is quite conventional and should not be difficult. The rudder is a little different in that it is made from two Lite-Ply facings with balsa spacers between them. The balsa parts will require some sanding in order to preserve the shape of the rudder, but this too will not be difficult to accomplish.

The Triplane is naturally a wing builders delight in that there are three of them to construct. There is a minor difficulty here due to the fact that the side view shows the ailerons in the center wing and the wing plans show the ailerons in the top wing. Documentation shows the top wing to be correct. This requires the mounting of the aileron servo in the top wing (also shown) and the use of an extension servo lead to reach it. (Check your radio to assure that this long lead does not create an interference problem).

The installation of the ailerons in the center wing, as shown on the side view of the fuselage, is detailed on the plans. But, it should not even be considered as it is totally out of scale!

All ribs are cap-stripped, top and bottom, so the builder can plan on spending considerable time cutting and installing cap strips. (As noted above, the Tripe is a wing builder's delight!)

All three wings are constant chord, although the top wing has a longer chord in its outer panels. This will mean making a few more wing ribs. All three wings are shown as one piece, and this should not present a problem in transporting them as they are relatively short, anyway.

The center wing removes along with a section of the top of the fuselage and the cabane struts. This is held in place with bolts tapped into hardwood blocks, and makes for an easy assembly at the flying field.

The landing gear and cabane wires are shown full sized on the plan and are neither complex nor difficult to bend. The gear track is rather narrow and this may cause the Triplane to be a bit of a 'handful' on the ground. Proper setup of the wheels will help alleviate some of the potential problem. This requires some 'toe-in' and for the wheels to have some 'camber' as well. (Wheels canted outward at the top.)

DEGREE OF DIFFICULTY:

Nothing here to give the experienced any difficulty. A newcomer should try something as little simpler first or have some experienced help handy. Our '3' rating tells it all.

1/4 SCALE

SOPWITH 'PUP'

FROM: Behren's Plan Service, 31-27 Healey Ave., Far Rockaway, N.Y. 11691

SPAN: 80" CHORD: 16" DOD: 4 AREA: 2300 Sq.In.

LENGTH: 58 " WEIGHT: Unspecified ENGINE: Quadra 35

HISTORICAL:

The Sopwith Pup which was originally intended to be called the Sopwith Scout, Mark something-or-other, so closely resembled its slightly larger relative, the 1 1/2 Strutter, that everyone began referring to it as the 'Pup'. Despite repeated (official) orders to the contrary, the name stuck, and Pup it's been ever since.

The Pup became an official entity on February 9th 1916. Sopwith, at that time, had contracts with the British Admiralty (Navy) and the first Pups were delivered to the Royal Naval Air Service.

Powered with an 80 HP Clerget rotary engine, the Pup became an immediate success. It's performance on the relatively limited horsepower was impressive and handling in the air, impeccable.

The Pup was fitted with a single Vickers machine gun mounted on the centerline of the fuselage, ahead of the cockpit. Several different interrupter (synchronizer) mechanisms were used at one time or another to protect the propeller from bullets.

The Pup, due to it's naval origins, was flown from shipboard in a variety of ways. Aside from more-or-less 'normal' operations from early aircraft carriers, Pups were flown from platforms mounted aboard lesser ships as well. One such platform (aboard the Light Cruiser HMS Yarmouth) provided a take-off run of but 20 feet. Recovery was not possible, for obvious reasons.

PLAN:

Behren's plans are sparse compared with the detail shown on most plans. While they are complete, and will permit construction of a flying model, the details many will expect are not present. The Sopwith Pup is shown on two plan sheets and the set comes with a construction pamphlet.

The plan departs from scale where convenient for simplified construction. The airfoil on the original aircraft was undercambered and both undercambered and flat- bottomed airfoils are shown; builder's choice.

Fuselage construction is 'stick' type and pine is called out as the material. Basswood or spruce could be used in its place. All fuselage joints are shown gussetted and the gussets should not be omitted. The crosspieces, which join the fuselage sides, are not shown gussetted. They should be!

There are a considerable number of formers required, so quite an amount of time will need to be spent in patterning and cutting parts.

Landing gear legs are made from music wire, which is then faired with balsa strips. Full sized patterns are on the plan sheets for the parts which go to make up the landing gear assembly. The tail skid is shown sprung, and some small parts will be required.

The cabane strut patterns are also shown and some skill will be required in bending the screw loops at their upper ends. These must take the screws which will hold the upper wing in place.

The firewall is shown as 1/4 inch stock and this is a little light for the recommended Quadra engine. Doubling the material size would be wise. (The added weight forward may be required anyhow, due to the short nose moment arm.)

Tail group members are framed from 'stick' material. All curved outer edges (including wing tip bows) are made from laminated strip material. Keep the tail feathers light, it would not be too difficult to come up with a tail-heavy model.

Only one wing panel is shown for the four required. It will be necessary to build two on the front of the plan and two on the back. The pamphlet shows alternate methods of mounting (and building) the upper wing, so a careful decision should be made here. (In the 1/3 scale kit, produced by Balsa USA, the upper wing center section is permanently mounted to the fuselage. Under these circumstances, it cannot get out of proper trim.)

Both front and rear wing spars are 'box' construction and will be quite strong. If this type of construction has not been used before, the builder is advised to assemble the spars carefully. Once completed, they should be carefully checked with a 'stock' wing rib, along their entire length, to assure that no problems will be encountered when the time comes to assemble the ribs to them.

While no rigging wires are shown on the plan, the flying surfaces are quite large and consideration should be given to making use them to provide greater strength. Besides, they're scale!

The interplane struts are made from 1/2 inch pine (or equivalent) and make quite ingenious use of Dubro ball and socket connectors to hold them in place. Over time, it has been the writer's experience that these connectors lose their hold and they may not be the best choice where they will be subject to continual assembly and disassembly.

DEGREE OF DIFFICULTY:

While the structures involved are not complex, there is a great deal of building required. Much of the work involves parts which appear too light for the job, so considerable care is required during construction. Our '4' indicates this model should be avoided by the very low-time builder.

21% FULL-SIZE

BEECHCRAFT STAGGERWING,G-17S

FROM: Lee Richter, 14026 Maple Ridge Rd., New Berlin, Wisconsin, 53151

SPAN: 80 1/2"   CHORD: 12 3/4"   AREA:1896 sq.in.

LENGTH: 70"   DOD: 5   WEIGHT: 22-28 #   ENGINE: Q35/ 50

HISTORICAL:

It would be difficult to find an airplane which better typifies "Classic" than the Beechcraft Staggerwing. Designed in an era when aircraft builders were not selling a great deal of product, the Staggerwing fought hard for it's share of the market and went through some hard years before getting Walter Beech and his company into the black.

Of the two best known Staggerwings, the 'D' model was built in the largest numbers. Many of these still survive in the hands of collectors. Most are either well restored or in the process of being reworked by their owners.

The Model 17 Beechcraft was ahead of its time. While not all Stags were capable of 200 MPH, many were, and the story still survives that they were all capable of such speeds. In truth, the Staggerwing was an airborne carriage of some considerable style. Capable of carrying five people and their baggage at speeds in the high one hundred's, the Staggerwing could, and did, show it's heels to military pursuit planes of the day. And with considerable comfort in that roomy closed cabin.

The subject of this plan is the 'G' Model, of which only 20 were built. A surprising number of these still exist although their numbers have declined significantly over the years. A restored 'D' Model is worth about $80,000 these days and the even rarer 'G' Model would fetch an even higher price, if one was available. The two models were very much alike, having the same basic dimensions. The 'G' Model's cowl flowed smoothly back into the fuselage, giving it a much sleeker look than the 'D' Model.

PLAN:

This plan is a first effort by Lee Richter with the help of Dario Brisighella. It is an excellent plan consisting of five plan sheets, with a sixth sheet detailing the retracting landing gear, for those who have the skills and facilities to do their own machining. Without retracts, the model lacks that finishing touch which separates the real beauty from the also-ran. No building booklet is available, all of the instructions required being lettered on the plans.

The fuselage sub-frame is called out as 1/4 square pine, but spruce or any of the common straight-grained soft woods could be used. Gussetting is shown at all fuselage joints and should not be omitted.

There are a goodly number of formers to be made up so quite a lot of pattern making, transferring, and parts cutting is required in order to build this impressive model.

Wing spars are 1/4 square spruce and webbing is applied right out to the last bay outboard, which makes for a very strong wing. The flying and landing wires are functional so some care is required in making up and installing the anchor points for these wires.

The Staggerwings had ailerons on the top wings and flaps on the bottom; both are shown on the plan. The flaps are the split trailing edge variety.

There are several rather complicated shapes to duplicate and a significant number of quite large parts to make, so this Staggerwing is not going to be a cheap, quick and dirty airplane to model. Fidelity to scale is excellent so the building of a highly competitive model is possible.

The sixth plan sheet, which shows the construction of a very prototypical retracting gear, is available as an option from the designer. This plan will permit the construction of a set of retracts which hew very closely to those of the original airplane. It might be possible to install a set of Byron retracts, but considerable work would be required. The gear legs from Byron should be installed even if they do not retract, just for their scale appearance.

The upper wing is built in one piece and two servos are shown, one for each aileron. The lower wing is built in two pieces, with the center section remaining on the fuselage. This permits the model to stand on it's own gear while being transported.

Flap servos are in each wing lower wing panel, requiring both 'Y' connectors and longer than normal servo leads. The elevator is split and thus requires two servos, one operating each half. This means there will be eight servos required to fly this airplane. Thus, it goes without saying that there will be a rather high battery consumption rate. So, a redundant battery system with two 1200 mah packs is almost mandatory.

Lee Richter's Beechcraft is a tour de force for a first time designer (even if he did have some expert help from Dario). The plan is very complete and builds a model which could be made into a very competitive scale model. It's good looks and the bonus flight points for mechanical options will make this model hard to beat in competition.

DEGREE OF DIFFICULTY:

NOT for the low time builder as there are some complicated shapes and structures to be made up, along with a wing set-up which requires functional landing and flying wires. For this reason, the newcomer should leave the Stag alone until he has had some building experience. The model flies well, but tends to be relatively fast in comparison to most biplanes. Not for the low time pilot.

1/4 SCALE

BOEING F4B-1 (THROUGH F4B-4)

FROM: JAN JANACEK, 2555 1/2 So. Judkins St., Seattle, WN. 98144

SPAN: 92" (Top) 74 3/4"(Bot) CHORD: 16" AREA: 1872 SQ.IN.

LENGTH: 61 1/2" WEIGHT: UNSPECIFIED DOD: 3 ENGINE: Q35

HISTORICAL:

One of the better known U.S. Navy Boeing biplane fighters of the early thirties, the first in the series was the F4B-I. Deliveries began in 1929. It was followed by the F4B-2 in 1931 and the F4B-3 in July of 1932. Ninety-two of the latter were delivered to the carriers Langley and Saratoga. The ultimate Boeing Navy biplane fighter, the F4B-4, was equipped with an R-1340 engine of 550 HP, giving it a speed of 188 MPH. The F4B-4's were armed with a pair of .30 caliber machine guns, or one .30 caliber and one 50 caliber.

The Army Air Corps version of the F4B-series were known as P-12's, in a variety of different configurations incorporating many modifications and minor alterations over the period of time the airplane was produced.

An all-metal version of the P-12 was funded by Boeing in the hopes of obtaining a contract with the

Army. Eventually 135 of the metal P-12's were built. The last 25 of the order were designated P-12F and had 600 HP engines installed. Other changes altered it's appearance quite markedly from that of the F4B-4.

Janacek's drawings note the details of the first F4B production version. However, there is so much documentation available on the Boeing biplane fighter, that it would be an easy task to "up-date" the F4B-1 model to any of the intermediate configurations up to the "dash-four" Navy version or any of the Army's P-12 series aircraft

PLAN:

The drawing consists of five plans sheets. (One sheet shows variations for the F4B-2.). The plan is well done and not overly difficult. No instructions are furnished. Some building from plans experience is assumed.

The fuselage is built-up framework with shaping formers assembled over the basic structure. Spruce is called out for almost all of the framing in the fuselage and all joints are shown with gussets. The structure is well designed and carefully thought out to provide great strength with light weight. While the wings are constant chord, there are still a large number of ribs to be made. The use of the 'stack' method will permit them to be made up several at a time. The fuselage formers are a variety of shapes and sizes so a large amount of pattern making and cutting will be required.

Only the top wings have ailerons, but the mechanism for operating them runs out through the bottom wing, then connects to the upper wing ailerons with a link strut. Care will need to be taken here, as the length of the mechanical linkage may induce considerable 'slop' or lost motion in the mechanism. It might be as well to re-design this arrangement to allow the aileron servo(s) to be placed in the upper wing. This will necessitate running the servo wires to the upper wing, but this could be arranged by running them up the cabane struts without their being too obvious. The upper wing is made in three sections as the center section remains in place and the outer sections plug into it.

The empennage (tail feathers) will present no problems; very straight-forward construction. If your experience with plans building is limited, beginning construction with the tail group is an excellent idea. It will provide an easy introduction to the requirements of plans building on a simple structure, rather than a complex one.

Care must be taken in rigging the finished model for flight. It would be quite possible to alter the wing positioning through tensioning the flying and landing wires and, if they are not rigged properly, some rather strange flight characteristics may be created.

Once assembled, any model should be set up on a flat plane (a concrete floor, for example) and then rigged so both wings (all four sections in the case of the F4B) are at the same relative position to one another and to the fuselage. The vertical fin should be checked at right angles to the horizontal stabilizer which, in turn, should be parallel to the wings. Care taken in making all of these set-ups as precise as possible will result in a model which has a better chance of flying properly.

DEGREE OF DIFFICULTY:

While there is a good deal of construction, most of it is quite simple and should not create any problems. As with any biplane, the construction of wings can be a chore. The rigging of the wings for flight will require some care as the landing and flying wires are functional.

COMMENTS:

Any one of the four airplanes can be duplicated from this plan. (F4B-1, -2 -3, -4). Good documentation is available from Squadron Publications (Nos. 2 and 27). Modern photographs are available of at least two restoration (the National Air and Space Museum owns a beautifully restored F4B-4 in Marine colors!).

1/4 SCALE

BUCKER JUNGMANN (BU 131)

C.A.P. PLAN FROM: Bob Holman Plans, P.O. Box 741, San Bernardino, Ca. 92402

SPAN: (BOTH) 72 3/4" CHORD: 10 1/2" DOD: 3 AREA: 1527 SQ. IN.

LENGTH: 66 1/2" WEIGHT: 10 3/4 # (W/.60) ENGINE: .60 TO .90

HISTORICAL:

The Bucker Jungmann was the predecesor of the better known Jungmeister. The Jungmann was used by the German Luftwaffe as a trainer during the 1930's.

Both the Jungmann and the Jungmeister ("Young Man" and "Young Master", respectively) are highly aerobatic, although the Jungmeister had the edge in competition. The two machines look very much alike with a very similar profile and both featured swept back wings. The Jungmann was usually powered by a Hirth in-line engine of 80 HP, later raised to 105 HP. The more popular Jungmeister used a radial engine. Some existing models of both aircraft have been re-engined with modern power plants.

The airplane had it's origins in Sweden, where Carl Bucker built aircraft during the years Germany was forbidden by the Treat of Versailles to do so. In 1932, Bucker moved back to Germany along with a talented Swedish Engineer, Lars Andersson. In 1934, they began building the Jungmann which was an immediate success and was chosen to equip the so-called 'sport' organization which began training what was to become the feared Luftwaffe.

The Jungmann, it was immediately apparent, was a very aerobatic machine. Its one flaw was its lack of adequate power for vertical maneuvers. A few Jungmann still exist and good photographic as well as three-view documentation is available.

The Jungmann was refined, re-powered and became the Bu 133 or Jungmeister, but that's a story for another plans page!

PLAN:

It has been said that English plans have the unhappy knack of being complex. That the English, faced with a choice, will always opt for the more complex, and usually more difficult, way of doing things.

That this may be true is not obvious from the Jungmann plan, designed by C.A.P. (Complete-A-Pac) who also have kits available for some of their offerings. Bob Holman at the above address will be able to provide more information.

Even in 1/4 scale, the Jungmann is not an overly large model. The span is just a touch over six feet, so it is a relatively small, "large" model. Power is suggested at .60 to .90 glow, which would be quite adequate to a model up to about 12 - 14 pounds. If a four stroker is decided upon, a slightly larger displacement engine would be more appropriate. Keep in mind that the narrow cowl of the Jungmann will require a somewhat narrow engine.

One complication to the construction of the Jungmann is the swept-back wings. The center section is straight, and the sweep-back begins at the outer edges of the center section. This requires a structure in which the spars in the center section and the spars in the outer panels are at an angle to one another. This makes for a tricky assembly both at the root of the outer panel and within the center section in order to provide the required wing center section strength. This also means the wing ribs are at an angle to the leading and trailing edges in order to be parallel to the airflow in flight.

The three plan sheets contain a quite comprehensive set of building instructions which, while brief, contain all the necessary information. One of the sheets is devoted entirely to the patterns for the parts, of which there are a bunch. Be prepared for an intense session of parts making.

The fuselage is a very sturdy structure, being well braced, and using formers at quite close intervals. Many of the formers are plywood and considerable bracing and gussetting is shown. The structure appears to be a good deal stronger than is really necessary with a glow engine mounted, and probably adds some unnecessary weight. This would not be a problem with an engine installed which was in the upper end of the recommended power range.

Engine mounts are shown as beam type which are not as common in North America as they are in Great Britain. No great problem should be encountered if this is changed to the more common radial mount.

The tail wheel is typically English, being held in place with epoxy smeared over a thread wrapping. It would be as well to change this to a stronger type of mount.

The model is claimed as 'stand-off' scale but a little research and some extra work could dress it up to do quite well in competition. Being a little out of the ordinary, it just might be that subject which would catch a judge's eye.

The Jungmann is not quite as attractive as the Jungmeister, but that is a subjective judgement. It is a little longer in the after fuselage than it's slightly smaller descendent, although many would not be able to tell them apart. The distinctive narrow cowl of the in-line engined Jungmann is the giveaway, of course.

At the upper end of the power range suggested, the model should fly very well and be capable of most aerobatic manuevers that the prototype Jungmann could manage. Properly flown, the Jungmann should do well in competition.

DEGREE OF DIFFICULTY:

The fuselage is built in two sections which requires some skill in making everything fit properly. While not overly complex, the parts for the Jungmann are smaller than the usual 1/4 and 1/3 scale models. The complicated structure within the wing center sections would provide some difficulty to the neophyte builder as well. A '3' on our rating scale.

1/4 SCALE

BUCKER JUNGMEISTER (BU 133)

FROM: RCM Plans, 144 W. Sierra Madre Blvd., Sierra Madre Ca. 91024

SPAN: 77"   CHORD 11 3/4"   AREA: 1770 Sq. In.

LENGTH: 68 1/2"   WEIGHT 20 - 26#   DOD: 3   ENGINE: .60 -.90

HISTORICAL:

The Bucker Jungmeister was developed from the Jungmann, which suffered somewhat from it's lack of power. In order to correct this deficiency, Chief Engineer Lars Andersson recalculated every load path throughout the structure of the Jungmann in order to provide the lightest possible weight with the greatest strength.

He also rebalanced the control system, including relocating some of the hinge points, in order to provide a control system which was both sensitive and not loaded with resistance. From this work came the Jungmeister's reputation for being able to anticipate a pilot's thought and react to it.

Data being collected on the Jungmann, which was still a fairly new aircraft, was also used in order to produce the 'Super Jungmann' which became the Jungmeister. What resulted from all this work was a slightly smaller airframe, which could withstand terminal velocity diving maneuvers and yet it weighed in, dry, at 925 pounds.

Once available, the Jungmeister never looked back. It won an aerobatic event at the Berlin Olympics of 1936, the only time aerobatics have ever been included as an event at the Olympics.

Of the approximately 600 Jungmeisters built, somewhere around thirty still survive, with about a dozen or so to be found in the U.S. Beverly (Bevo) Howard's is in the Smithsonian, restored by a group of his friends after it crashed, taking his life.

Just keep things straight -- if it has an in-line engine, it's a Jungmann. If the engine's "round", it's a Jungmeister!

PLAN:

The RCM plan is about what we have come to expect of RCM. It is well done, well thought out, and is available as a kit as well (from Pica). The plan is on two sheets and, when ordered from RCM, comes with a copy of the article published with it.

Much as with the Jungmann covered on an earlier page, the Jungmeister has the swept back wing which leads to a few problems when aligning and assembling the model.

There are a number of patterns to transfer to material and a part to make for each of them. None of the parts should be difficult to make as the shapes are all quite simple.

Take care making up the cabane struts as any inaccuracies here can create problems later when trimming the bird for flight. An angle of incidence of minus one degree is recommended. This could be shimmed to a different incidence later if it is felt such a change will improve flying characteristics.

The designer has shown beam engine mounts in the model and they are accommodated by notches in three of the formers. If you should decide to use a metal radial motor mount, these cut-outs should be eliminated. The plan also favors a fuel tank which resides just behind the engine within the cowling area. This is a good idea as it provides ready access to the tank and fuel lines without having to dig inside the fuselage. The tank may be easily removed if the engine is first unbolted.

The tail surfaces are built up on a balsa sheet base, with partial ribs on each side. This provides great rigidity to these surfaces and will prevent them from warping with every change in temperature and humidity. The core material is 1/8" balsa.

At the weight specified, using a .60, the performance of this model will be a great deal less than prototypical. It is recommended that as large an engine as will conveniently fit in the cowling be used. It will turn the model into the sparkling performer that its full sized counterpart was.

The Jungmeister at Quarter Scale is also a small, "large" model. The one piece wings of just under six-and-a-half feet are not a real chore to transport and the entire model is not unduly large. There is only one servo shown for ailerons, which means it will be moving four of them. A second servo, included in the early stages of construction, will halve the load on the aileron servo and is a good idea.

A redundant battery system is an accessory which should be considered for any scale model. It has the advantage of providing battery 'back-up' which can save a model, especially if you are inclined to push your luck a little with 'just one more flight'!

The engineering of the Jungmeister plan is such that few if any changes should be considered. As for documentation, there is a good deal available.

If you opt for the kit, it includes a three view as well as other documentation data. As noted above, Bevo Howard's machine is in the National Air & Space Museum where it may be photographed. Most of the scale documentation and photo-pack dealers have information on this Jungmeister due to it's popularity.

Quite a number of colorful paint schemes can be documented, what with the Jungmeister's ability as an airshow mount. A search should turn up a scheme to satisfy almost anyone.

Nice agile model for fun flying and could easily be turned into a useable scale contest airplane.

DEGREE OF DIFFICULTY:

On our scale of five, the RCM Jungmeister is a three. There is a good deal of construction as with any biplane and the cabane strut area can be a bit hard to get just right, but there should be no great difficulty for anyone who has plans-built, or who has built several models from kits.

1/3 SCALE

BUCKER JUNGMEISTER (BU 133)

FROM: Giuseppe Fantini, Via G. Daneo 31-16, 16144 Genoa, Italy

SPAN: 89.7" CHORD: 13.25" DOD 4-5 AREA: 2251 Sq.In.

LENGTH: 79" WEIGHT: 18# ENGINE: 1.2 c.i. or larger

HISTORICAL:

See details in the preceding Bucker Jungmeister write-up.

PLAN:

Giuseppe Fantini's plan is included here due to it's rather spectacular size. At 1/3 scale, it's a large model although a span of just under 90 inches is not so large as to be a real problem to move around.

This drawing by Fantini has a few problems. All of the written data on the plan is in Italian! A subtle drawback if you do not read Italian or have a friend who does. The plan in the author's collection has been annotated with very brief English translations of some of the material printed on it. Even without this limited translation, a capable model builder could produce a beautiful Bucker from Fantini's drawing. Any sizes called out on the plan are in metric measure, of course.

The fuselage is built-up. The material is 6 mm, but 1/4 square could be used with little difficulty. The material called out is Obeche wood, which is not readily available in North America, so spruce would be an acceptable substitute. All fuselage joints are shown gussetted, which is a practice the authors have been recommending for years. Leaving the gussets out should not even be considered.

The cowling is quite large and is built-up. It us highly unlikely you'll find the appropriate cowl from North American accessory suppliers. The size of the cowling would permit almost any available engine to be installed.

With this large a biplane, and all that drag, aerobatic performance would only be attained with plenty of reliable power up front! (The engine shown is described as 22 cc, turning an 18 X 6 propeller. The engine is not identifiable from the plan (10 cc is equal to a .60, so 22 cc is about a 120, rather "puny" for this large a model.)

The landing gear is nicely engineered and is pivoted where it joins the fuselage and held in place by spring tension. It is not clear if this is prototypical, but it does look very good in the plan.

The cabane struts are screwed in place. This appears to make assembly and disassembly of the model easier than if it had fixed cabanes. The method of doing this appears quite strong and shows no signs of potential weakness.

Some of the structure appears to be rather light by North American standards, but using slightly larger wood sizes should be considered, depending on the power being used. With lots of wing area, good power would provide exciting aerobatic performance. The model would be somewhat light at 18 pounds, a weight unlikely to be held if a larger engine were used.

The airfoil used is an NACA 2412 modified, which is a semi-symmetrical section. It has a rather shallow entry so its induced drag should be minimal.

Servos are shown mounted at the aileron in the lower wings, which requires rather long servo leads. Be sure any sections of extension lead are securely connected where they are not accessible. You know what Murphy's Laws say about connections where you can't get at them! Also, check your radio for noise rejection from these long leads. Use chokes, Ace Noise Traps, or some sort of noise protection if there is any doubt about your radio's ability to reject the "noise".

Here again, a larger than the usual 500 mah battery must be used. Two 1200 mah packs operating through a redundant battery system would be a good idea.

The landing and flying wires are functional, of course, in anything this big. Be sure they will withstand the loads you'll place on them before flying the model. If there is any reason to doubt the integrity of the airplane, DON'T FLY IT.

There is some very interesting construction techniques in this Fantini Bucker. You'll have to make some metal parts for the bird, although these do not look very difficult to fabricate. Many of the anchor points for wires are made up from wood screws whose heads require reshaping. Do not try to screw them into balsa wood! Make sure they're securely anchored into ply or hard wood.

In summary: There are some innovative construction method on this plan. They aren't in general use in North America, and. There is no doubt that Fantini's drawings will produce a striking model at 1/3 scale. If you find you are able to have the printed material on the plan translated, you'll probably find this a relatively easy project if you have plansbuilt previously. But even without a translation, the competent model builder should be able to produce a flyable (and impressive) model from Fantini's plan.

DEGREE OF DIFFICULTY:

Due to the lack of English language instructions, we have to suggest this model is a bit more difficult than a 3, but not so much as to be a 4. It is not a project for the beginner, especially at this size. If you have done some plans building in the past, and can read drawings well, building this GIANT model should be within your capabilities.

1/4 SCALE

CURTISS HAWK P-6E

FROM: Wendell Hostetler, 1041 Heatherwood Lane, Orrville, Ohio. 44667

SPAN: 84" CHORD: 15 3/4" Root, 9 5/8" Tip AREA: 1798 Sq. In.

LENGTH: 63 1/2" WEIGHT: 24-26# DOD: 4 ENGINE: 2 TO 5 HP

HISTORICAL:

The P-6 series of biplane fighters went through the most sweeping changes of any of the between-the-wars fighters. There were many variants including some racing biplanes, but these were not true fighters, using contoured cooling tubes mounted on the wings. Great for reducing drag, but too vulnerable for a fighter, subject to hostile action.

Only 46 P-6E's were built at a cost of $12,360 each. A far cry from today's multi-million dollar fighter aircraft.

Powered by a 600 HP V-1570C Conqueror V-type liquid cooled engine, the P-6E could make good just a hair under 200 MPH at sea level. Service Ceiling was 24,700 feet. Dry, the airplane tipped the scales at 2699 pounds and laden at 3392 pounds. Fuel capacity was 50 gallons internally and another 50 externally. Range, with 100 gallons on board, was 572 miles.

The P-6E was armed either with one .30 and one .50 caliber machine gun or two .50's. One of these machines, designated the XP-6H, had four extra .30 caliber guns mounted, two in the upper wing and two in the lower.

Span of the original airplane was 31 feet 6 inches, length 23 feet 2 inches, and height 8 foot 10 inches.

Many colorful paint schemes were used, typical of the era, and many of these are preserved in available documentation. At least one surviving example of the breed is on display at the USAF Museum at Wright-Patterson AFB, Dayton, Ohio. With the wide selection of variants and the many color schemes, there should be something available for every taste.

PLAN:

The Hostetler plan consists of two plans sheets and an instruction manual. As is usual with his plans, this one is un-cluttered, but contains such detail as is necessary for construction.

The engine shown on the plans sheets is the 2.44 c.i. Kioritz. along with a shock mounting method developed and used frequently by Hostetler. This method utilizes rubber tubing through which the engine mounting bolts pass and it appears to be an excellent vibration reducing system.

T & D Fiberglass has a cowling, wheel pants and an external 'slipper' type drop tank for the P-6E. There is just adequate room inside the cowling to take the Kioritz engine.

Fuselage construction is quite conventional stick structure using formers and longerons to provide the correct shape of the model. The tail group is made up from 3/8" balsa stock and is also made removable, if desired.

Cabane struts could readily be made removable. This makes the use of an 'envelope' for covering the fuselage with one piece of Dacron, Sig Koverall, or polyester a much easier task than if the cabanes had to remain in place. See Dick Phillips' "Building Big Is Beautiful" book for details on this covering method.

There are a few small metal parts to be made up, but none of these should cause the builder any problems.

Wing construction is quite conventional, although there is a good deal of it with both wings being built in one piece. A servo mounting area is shown in the center of the lower wing. This creates a slight problem in that the lower ailerons are smaller than the upper and the shorter lever arm provides minimal movement to the upper ailerons.

There are two other aileron mounting choices available. The aileron servos may be mounted in the upper wing which will require running the servo wire leads up the cabane struts from the receiver inside the fuselage. Alternately, servos could be mounted in both wings and upper and lower ailerons would be driven by separate servos. This method will require a dummy aileron connector rod that would have no function but cannot be omitted for appearance's sake.

On the smaller three views referred to for information on the P-6E, it appears that the aileron coupling link may have been mounted ahead of the hinge line on the lower aileron and this would have provided equal movement to both upper and lower ailerons.

The wing presents a few difficulties for the low time builder. The trailing edges are scalloped and this must be done accurately if it is to look good. In the original airplane, the trailing edge was made from wire. When covered and doped, the shrinkage of the material pulled the covering into short arcs between the wing ribs. It's not the easiest thing to duplicate in wood.

Another treatment not always seen is used in order to build a 'true' and accurate wing using either symmetrical or semi-symmetrical wing ribs. Hostetler shows all ribs with a 'keel-piece' on them in order for them to sit properly on the building board while the wing is being constructed. These are subsequently cut off, and the ribs sanded to contour. These pieces must be accurately cut or the wing will not be true. Care is required here to see that they are made correctly, and removed carefully.

This is a good plan, making up into a striking and attractive model. Good scale subject, and colorful when finished properly. Flies very well on the power shown and looks very good in the air. An excellent scale subject.

DEGREE OF DIFFICULTY:

Lots of building here and a lot of accurate and precise work needed to mount the upper wing properly. Thus, our rating of a 4 for difficulty of construction.

1/4 SCALE

FAIRCHILD 22 C7A

FROM: BOB FLORENCE, 23721 Lake Drive East, Bothell, Washington, 98021

SPAN: 101" CHORD: 15 1/2" DOD: 3 AREA: 1565 Sq. In.

HISTORICAL:

The first "Fairchild 22" appeared in 1931 as the Kreider-Reisner model C-7. A two-place parasol monoplane, it was first powered by an 80 Hp Genet radial engine. In the hands of Fairchild, it soon sported in-line engines of 75 (Michigan-Rover) to 95 (American Cirrus) horsepower, along with slim fuselage contours in production versions. Since it was "aimed" at the "sportsman pilot", who demanded more performance than the in-lines would give, substantial modifications were made and Warner engines of 125 and 145 horsepower were installed.

The change to these "round engines" resulted in a redesign of the 22's fuselage to a more efficient, though heftier-appearing streamlined shape. While they were at it, Fairchild engineers added wheel pants and drag-reducing "cuffs" to the ends of the host of struts. They turned it into a beautiful bird.

The 22 spanned 32 feet, ten inches, (NACA N-22 airfoil); was 22 feet long and 7 feet, 11 inches high. Max speed was 130 and it cruised at 110 (125 Warner version). It could be equipped with Edo floats.

PLAN:

Another example of the co-operation between Jan Janacek and Bob Florence, this plan for the Fairchild 22 is an excellent one. The three plan sheets are clean and clear. No builder's manual is included, but there is nothing here to give an experienced builder any trouble.

The model's construction is quite conventional. Sides are framed up over the plan, then joined with cross-pieces. All of the structural material is called out as spruce, with the main longerons being 3/8 square. All bays aft of the front cockpit are diagonally braced and all fuselage joints are gusseted. This fuselage has been extremely well designed and is strong!

There is a minor inconsistency in the formers. Formers B3, A and B, and formers B4, A and B are shown as being identical. As the 'B' formers are mounted at an angle, this cannot be correct as they will need to be slightly larger than the 'A' formers in order to fit properly. This should be taken into account when the formers are being made.

The fuselage is flat sided and the finished shape is attained through the use of two stringers running the full length of the fuselage.

A half inch firewall is shown to which the Quadra engine mount is attached -- also good practice. (Millmount shown.)

The tail group is made up of stick construction with a laminated strip outline. Control surfaces are generous as is usually the case with older airplanes, thus providing excellent control in the air.

The wing is built in three sections with the center section fastened to the cabane struts. The main wing panels use box spars front and rear so the wing is an exceptionally strong one. The center section has protruding hardwood spars which are housed inside the box spars in the wing sections. The wings are retained in position by 4-40 bolts passing through both the solid and the box spar, nesting in a blind nut. The bolts are inserted from the bottom so they will not be noticeable.

The airfoil used is the Navy N-22, and, as the wing is constant chord, only one basic wing rib is required. Two servos are shown for the ailerons, one in each wing. The ailerons are relatively narrow, but they stretch from the center section to the tip so they will be quite effective.

The wing struts are functional and should be made and fitted with care. With the type of wing construction used, the struts will not be heavily loaded, but they should not be neglected. They are necessary for flight.

Some metal working ability will be required as there are some small fittings to be made for the strut connection to the landing gear. There are actually three struts and a shock to be made, to duplicate the rather complex arrangement on the original airplane. Some skill and ingenuity will be required to make up the smaller parts necessary in order to preserve the integrity and strength of the mechanical arrangement shown.

Some documentation information is included on the plan sheets, indicating where photographs of the airplane may be found. It also details the ownership of one such Fairchild still flying.

An interesting and unique model is possible from this plan set, one not seen at every model flying field in the country. At a weight of between 20 and 24 pounds, it should fly very well indeed. These weights would result in wing loadings of 29 to 35 ounces per square foot respectively, well within reasonable limits for such a model.

DEGREE OF DIFFICULTY:

While basically consisting of quite straight-forward construction, the strut hardware and inter-connection between the landing gear and the struts, plus making the shock absorber will provide some interesting and moderately difficult hand work. Thus our '3' rating, perhaps leaning a little toward a '4'.

1/4 SCALE

GYPSY MOTH

FROM: Model Builder Plans Service, 621 W. 19th St., Costa Mesa, Calif., 92627

SPAN: 90" CHORD: 13" DOD: 4 AREA: 2150 Sq. In.

LENGTH: 70" WEIGHT: 12 - 14# ENGINE: .60

HISTORICAL:

The de Haviland 'Moth' airplanes should need no introduction to anyone interested in aircraft history. The series began in the twenties with the DH 60 Moth and went on to become the better known Tiger Moth. The 'Tiger' trained literally thousands of Allied pilots during WWII, and many still fly.

The original Moths achieved world wide fame and sales records. They were copied by many other manufacturers, all being able to appreciate success. It has been said that the de Haviland Moth was the instrument which provided for the birth of the light airplane movement. Certainly this is true of Great Britain.

The Gypsy Moth appeared in 1928, powered by the Gypsy engine of either 100 or 120 horse-power. De Haviland went on to produce many variants, powered with a variety of engines of their own manufacture (and others).

Chief difference among this wide variety of aircraft was the engine installed. The engine required alterations in the cowling (principally in the upper half) in order to accommodate the size and shape of the engine used. Careful work documenting the aircraft being modeled will be required in order to produce an accurate scale model. This work should be done prior to the start of any construction, of course. There are still many **Tiger Moths** extant. There are not so many **Gypsy Moths**.

PLAN:

Model Builder's plan is on two sheets and was designed by publisher Bill Northrop and flown in an early R/C Nats. A photo still exists of this pioneering effort showing Bill flying the model using a transmitter sitting on the ground beside him. (That's the way it used to be, transmitters were too big and too heavy to hold!)

The authors have seen several Moths fly (not knowingly one from this particular plan) and they have all been gentle and easy machines to control. The trick is in knowing what the original airplane could do and then flying the model in an appropriate manner.

At the time of the construction of Northrop's original model, the .60 was the top of the line. In light of recent development, it might be as well to use a larger engine even at the weight specified. A four-cycle engine of .90 to 1.20 size would be chosen by the writer.

Fuselage construction is quite conventional stick building which will give no trouble to anyone with plans building experience. Most parts are quite simple to make and only the turtledeck formers are curved.

The cowling is made from balsa block material, hollowed out inside to provide adequate room for the engine. The rough shape is built up from several small balsa blocks (glued together) and then shaped to suit the cowling required.

The tail feathers show the classic de Haviland fin and rudder. Their outlines and those of the stabilizer are laminated from strip stock. The remainder of the rudder and elevator outline is cut from flat sheet stock.

The rudder and elevator are shown controlled by cables as was the case in the original airplane. The rudder bar, for example, projects through the sides of the cockpit and cables run from it's ends to the rudder horn. Elevator control is also by cable.

The wings are constant chord, so a minimum of ribs is required. The wings are a bit tricky to make because there is some taper required in the spars and the wing planform is somewhat irregular in shape. Careful building will preclude any problems here.

The wing is under-cambered so will provide some fun in covering. While this can be tricky, it is quite possible to make the covering adhere to the under-cambered ribs and stay there. Eighty false ribs are required and their placement will provide some rather tedious work.

Wing spars were specified as 3/16 by 1/2 inch balsa. This could readily be altered to spruce with a minimal weight penalty, especially if a little more power were to be used in place of the engine recommended. These spars were webbed more than half their span so will provide quite adequate strength.

The rigging shown is all functional and must not be omitted. This includes the rigging on the cabane struts. It should not be left out in any case for it's appearance value.

Ailerons are on the lower wing only and a servo is shown for each wing (the wings demount from the fuselage as four sections). These need not be particularly strong servos as the Moth is a gentle flyer and should not tear up the sky as if it were a pattern model.

A novel (for today) method of hinging is shown for all control surfaces and it should provide controls which move of their own weight, providing little resistance to control deflection.

DEGREE OF DIFFICULTY:

While we have assigned a '4' to the Gypsy Moth, we lean a little toward a '3' in this judgement. There are some slight difficulties in the model, but they are few and relatively minor. A superb scale model is possible from this plan. Flight of the model will be gentle and attractive.

1/4 SCALE

PIPER J-3 CUB

FROM: Sid Morgan Plans, 13157 Ormond, Belleville, Michigan. 48111

SPAN: 108"   CHORD: 16 1/2   DOD: 2   AREA: 1780 Sq. In.

LENGTH: 68 1/2"   WEIGHT: 14 -18#   ENGINE:.90 - 2.0

HISTORICAL:

Mr. Piper's ubiquitous 'Cub' hardly needs any introduction to anyone who knows anything about airplanes. This high winged monoplane trainer has been around for so long, almost everyone has seen one, ridden in one, or at least seen photos of one.

The number of pilot's licenses which have been issued as a result of training in the J-3 is undoubtedly long and contains many well known names.

The Cub has undergone a number of changes since the J-1 first appeared and began the chain of events which has seen Piper become one of the leading producers of civil airplanes in the world.

The Cub has been used by the military, including such volunteer outfits as the C.A.P. and has seen service, both civil and military, in almost every part of the world.

The Cub has had it's wings clipped for better aerobatic performance; that of Hazel Sig/Hester being among the better known of this particular breed.

Good documentation is available from many of the firms specializing in such material, including three-views and numerous photo-packs. In many cases, all that's required is a trip to the local airport, camera in hand. Cubs have been painted in as many colors as can be imagined, but the standard 'Cub Yellow' is the most readily recognized. Also see; Air Progress, Dec. 1969 and Fall 1960 for additional details useful in documenting the J-3 for scale contest work.

PLAN:

This 1/4 scale Morgan plan was the first model ever flown on a Quadra engine, in 1975. The model was built by one of the authors and is credited with having started the large model movement. While this is partly true, in relation to the engine used, many people were building large models long before there were really suitable engines available to fly them. Some were doing so long before the advent of radio control.

This J-3 plan was developed in 1971 by Bob Sweitzer and has been available for many years through Sid Morgan Plans. The three sheet plan is well done and includes all details necessary to build the model. All construction is quite conventional and will give anyone with any building experience no trouble.

The fuselage is stick stock and, while balsa is called out on the plan, switching this material to spruce and gusseting all fuselage joints will provide a model which will be very strong indeed. These alterations will increase the weight, of course, and the model can be built at the lower end of the specified weight if built as shown on the plan. However, if a large gas-fueled engine is to be used, the changes are recommended. (The author's J-3 weighed 16 pounds and was flown using the Quadra 35 engine, all that was available at the time.)

All fuselage formers are shown full sized and, as there are no curved surfaces, all may be cut accurately with considerable ease. The only place which requires any real attention to detail is the area of the cabin top. This area incorporates the wing mounting structure and requires care in assuring that proper glue joints are made and that all parts fit well. Many of these mounting tongue parts are interlocking so should be checked for proper fit as they are made. Note that the cabin top may be made removable for access to the interior of the cabin if desired.

With the advent of larger glow engines, and especially four cycle engines, the lighter construction will be quite adequate. (Note: 1/32 plywood gussets will add minimal weight and considerable strength and are recommended for ALL scale models.)

The landing gear is bent from 3/16 inch wire and is quite simple. No problems should be encountered making up the gear.

Empennage parts are built up from stick stock and are quite conventional construction. The tail group outlines are cut from sheet stock, so some transferring of patterns and parts cutting is required here. Nothing at all of any difficulty whatsoever.

The wing panels are both shown on the plan and are built as separate assemblies. The wings are held to the fuselage by a 'box' structure which is part of the wings. The cabin top has a tongue which fits into the box. The tongues are then retained in place with screws, inserted from the bottom of the wing, out of sight. This is a very strong mounting but as the struts are working struts they must be made up with this need in mind. (The author once had a wing strut fail in flight. The box/tongue arrangement permitted the model to be landed without damage, despite the loss of the strut on one side.)

Aileron servos are shown in both wings, mounted at the inboard end of the aileron. This is an excellent solution to the problem of control 'slop' inherent in long control linkages. However, it is well to arrange for access to such servos.

DEGREE OF DIFFICULTY:

Our '2' indicates we believe this J-3 to be an easy model to construct. While no instruction booklet is available, the plan does contain enough detail for the low-time builder to create a fine looking, good flying, J-3.

1/3 SCALE

PIPER J-3 CUB

FROM: Cedarbridge Scale, RR #4, Creemore, Ontario, Canada. L0M 1G0

SPAN: 140 7/8" CHORD: 22 1/2" DOD: 5 AREA: 3100 Sq. In.

LENGTH: 88 7/8" WEIGHT: 30# ENGINE: Quadra 35

HISTORICAL:

SEE PREVIOUS J-3 LISTING.

PLAN:

World scale champion Bob Nelitz has created the ultimate J-3 with these two very large plan sheets for his 1/3 scale Cub. The model created from this plan is VERY large, wingspan is just under 12 feet.

The plan is extremely well done and seeks to duplicate, in every way possible, the original airplane. Photographs of the prototype model are difficult to tell from full scale.

The fuselage is made mainly from dowel stock, approximating the tubing used in the original. Obviously, this work will require considerable care and accuracy in order to keep the dowel material in proper position.

The Cub fuselage is not a complex structure, but considerable care will be required in order to duplicate the original. A number of metal parts will be needed to make the model so some skill with small metal parts making will be a definite advantage.

A sub-assembly, made up from 5/16 inch steel tubing, is required in the cabin area to which the wing is attached. This must be accurately made in order to fit inside the cabin area.

The landing gear is welded from tubing as well and will require some skill in metal working. Several small parts are needed here. Particularly in the 'bungee' shock absorber.

The Quadra 35 engine was used in the prototype and provided quite adequate power for prototypical performance. The original model has towed a large banner off the ground on take-off so excess power is available from the relatively small engine.

Tail group members are also made to closely resemble the full scale airplane. Square spruce and dowel stock are used. Hinges in the tail group are made from brass tubing and require a nylon bushing and bolt to provide the pivot point. Outer edges of the stabilizer, elevator and wingtip are made from 3/8 inch dowel which is soaked for 8 hours prior to being bent to the necessary shape.

The stabilizer is rigged so as to be adjustable as in the full scale airplane. This adjustment is accessible after completion in order to adjust the stab incidence for best flight characteristics.

The plan shows only one wing panel so the other will need to be built on the back of the oiled plan sheet. Wing structure follows the original in all respects and will require additional metal parts fabrication for the aileron hinges, jury strut mounting hardware and strut mounts.

Wing spars are made from spruce stock; the front spar being 5/16 X 1 1/4 inches and the rear, 5/16 X 3/4 inch. This material will need to be selected with care due to it's length. Some shaping is needed in these parts. The wing ribs are slotted and slip onto the spars. Main strut and jury strut mounting plates are added during wing construction. A servo is shown in each wing (at the root rib) and the long control run to the bellcrank and aileron will require some care to keep 'slop' to a minimum.

The clipped wing version of the Cub is shown on the wing plan, although some 'horse-back' engineering will be needed to make the conversion.

Some attention to detail will be needed when the model is substantially complete and ready for rigging. This large model will need to be carefully rigged (as detailed on the plan sheets) before flight is attempted.

DEGREE OF DIFFICULTY:

While the J-3 Cub is generally looked upon as an 'easy' model, the Nelitz Cub should be attempted ONLY by the dedicated scale modeler. Our '5' indicates the close attention to detail required.

1/4 SCALE

1933 KINNER SPORTSTER MODEL 'K'

FROM: DGA Designs, 135 East Main St., Phelps, New York. 14532

SPAN: 117" CHORD: 17 5/8" DOD: 3 AREA: 2100 Sq. In.

LENGTH: 72.5" WEIGHT: 25 # ENGINE: Quadra 35

HISTORICAL:

Bert Kinner was, originally, a manufacturer of reliable "round engines" that powered a host of the three-seat biplanes in the late 20's and early 30's. In 1931 he became fascinated with folding wing lightplanes. He developed a pair of "folders" for the former "Bolte" sport plane and, together with Max B. Harlow, redesigned it into the Kinner Sportsman K. A low-winged, two place (side by side) monoplane, the 'K' had a five-cylinder Kinner K-5 engine.

The prototype was first shown in the 1932 Detroit Air Show -- with a three-toned purple paint job! Production of the Sportster continued through 1936 at the Kinner plant in Glendale, California.

Remarkably rugged, the 'K' served as a

sport plane as well as a trainer. It spanned 39 feet over its foldable wings (Clark Y airfoil, 0 degrees of incidence, 4.5 degrees of dihedral); was 23 feet, eight inches long; and cruised at a respectable 95 mph (Max: 105).It had a 300 mile range, while burning only 7 gallons of gas per hour. The 13,000-foot ceiling of the "K" was demonstrated by a "stunt". One was landed and taken off from a small plateau near the summit of Mt. Rainier in Washington state.

PLAN:

Four plan sheets and a building manual make up this excellent set. The model was designed from the last flying specimen of the Kinner (located in Hamburg, New York) and the designer offers both a three-view and a photo pack of the original as an optional extra. The plan is also available as a 2" = 1' (1/6th Scale) plan for those who'd rather build small.

There is also a fiberglass cowling and a landing gear set available; ordering details on the plan sheets.

The plan sheets are very well done, clear and concise and well laid out. The building booklet is a great help in completing construction. With the possible exception of making the parts necessary, building the Kinner will not be much different from building a well-designed kit.

The fuselage is simple stick construction. The joints are all gusseted with 1/32 inch plywood, always a good move. The forward part of the fuselage is doubled with a 1/16 inch plywood doubler for strength in this area. The fuselage shape is maintained by formers, of which there are quite a number so some pattern making and parts cutting is required. These are well detailed on the plans sheets so should present no difficulty.

The landing gear is a little out of the ordinary and incorporates a spring loaded shock absorber which will certainly add to the realism of the model and ease landings on rough ground. All landing gear parts are shown full size in their appropriate places. There is little wire bending that will create any problem. The shock absorber will require some metal working, but will not tax the abilities of those with some experience in this area. The wide stance landing gear will provide excellent ground handling for the Kinner.

Tail feathers are stick construction except that the curved outer edges are made up from laminated strip stock in all cases. As with most older airplanes, control surfaces are generous and the Kinner is claimed to be quite readily controllable right down to very slow speeds.

The rather long wing panels are built separately and each contains the servo operating its aileron. Good practice! The aileron control linkage uses arrow shaft for the pushrod, also good practice. As with any long mechanical linkage, care should be taken to eliminate any lost motion or 'slop'. The less there is, the less the control surface is likely to flutter and create problems in flight. The left wing panel, being a reverse of the same mylar from which the right wing plan was produced, assures complete accuracy.

The wing ribs are cap-stripped which makes for a fine looking finished product. It does take time to cut and fit all those cap strips, but the results are certainly worth the time it takes to do them. Wing tips are laminated from strip stock and then sanded to shape.

The center section of the wing is built as part of the fuselage which is quite convenient. When the model is being transported, the fuselage is able to stand on it's own gear rather than requiring a cradle to hold it in place. Electrical connection access to the aileron servos in the wings is cleverly concealed beneath the wing walk which is removed to gain access to the connectors. This too is handy in that an electrical connection is less likely to get out of adjustment than a mechanical one. Ailerons are quite large and will provide excellent control in flight.

DEGREE OF DIFFICULTY:

The Kinner will make an excellent model and a good introduction to plans building. The instructions are complete and will lead even the low time builder through the building process. Almost anyone with a kit or two under his belt will be able to produce a fine sport scale model from this plan. Thus our '3' which leans toward a '2'.

1/4 SCALE

MONOCOUPE 110 SPECIAL (CLIPPED-WING)

FROM: Classic Airplans, 321 Camelia Dr., Auburn, AL, 36830

SPAN: 95 " **CHORD: 14 7/8"** **DOD: 3** **AREA: 1428 Sq. In.**

LENGTH: 58 1/2" **WEIGHT: Unspecified** **ENGINE: .90 Glow**

HISTORICAL:

There's a lot more in the name of an aircraft than most of us realize. In the case of the Monocoupe the product of the Mono Aircraft Co. of Moline, Ill., the 'Mono' comes from the single wing (a monoplane); the 'coupe' comes from the fact that it was a two-place, side-by-side aircraft with two doors -- like an automobile 'coupe'. The 110 indicates that the aircraft was powered by a 110 Hp Warner radial.

The Monocoupe design first saw the light of day in 1928, as an enclosed aircraft equipped with a Velie engine. By 1935, it had evolved into the 90A, with its full cowling and streamlined wheel pants. Span was 32 feet (with a Clark "Y" airfoil, a favorite of us model builders!), length was 20 ft. 6" and maximum speed was a commendable 130 mph. That put it into a great number of 'stock' airplane races. Clipping its wings and adding engines of greater horsepower turned the 90A airframe into an out and out racer, or a spectacular aerobatic performer. As presented by A. Lynn Lockrow, the 110 Special duplicates the 23-foot clipped wing version. Approximately 10 airframes were modified to this configuration by their owners and the **factory**. Even in pure stock form, the 90A did a more than credible roll or loop.

PLAN:

This three sheet plan (no manual) from Classic Airplans is well done and a good deal closer to scale than a similar published plan. The model is 'stand-off' scale but is very close to the original. One plan sheet consists of details of the original airplane which will aid in making the model more realistic.

Fuselage is conventional construction, although the short transition from the round cowling to the rectangular fuselage takes place in a very short distance. This area will require some attention to get it right. The nose moment is quite short, so care should be taken to keep the tail feathers light. Any extra weight aft will require balance weight forward and such weight, while absolutely necessary, contributes nothing to the performance of the model.

It is recommended that the door of the model be made functional so that you may reach inside the fuselage. Wing hold-down bolts can, thus, be hidden inside (the reverse of normal construction procedures -- with the threaded maple blocks glued into the wing rather than to the fuselage).

As the engine is glow fuelled, there is not much need to alter any of the fuselage construction materials. Using spruce for the main longerons and gusseting the fuselage joints will create a much stronger model with a minimal weight penalty however.

A number of formers will be required although these are quite small and will not be a problem, nor consume much material. The main fuselage structure is not at all complicated, so should not be a problem for the experienced builder.

The landing gear is an aluminium blank, which is then covered with balsa fairings and shaped. Fastening such dissimilar materials together reliably is a difficult task and a good method of doing so has been detailed in the VIP book, "Building Big Is Beautiful".

Tail members are quite conventional in construction and will not take long to build. The elevator and fin outline are made up from laminated sheet stock and should be very strong.

The wing is built in three pieces and then assembled into one. The center section is flat and dihedral exists from the center section outboard. Only one wing panel is shown, so it will be necessary to build the other wing on the back of the plan.

The principal difference between the 90A and the 110 Special is the length of the wing panels. The shorter wing of the 110 is shown. The 110 wing is dramatically shorter than that of the 90A, so the area is also reduced by a significant amount. This will raises the wing loading appreciably and a larger engine may be opted for. A four-stroke engine in the 1.20 range would be an excellent choice.

The wing is constant chord almost to the tip so only a few wing ribs are needed. Ribs are capstripped, which makes for a good looking wing if done properly.

The spars are 1/4 X 3/8 inch spruce and although no webbing is shown, some vertical grained webbing trapped between the upper and lower spars will add considerable strength to the wing. (This need not run all the way to the tip.)

The airplane had both ailerons and flaps and these are shown on the plan. However, no servo location or control runs are illustrated. The center section of the wing has a sky-light, so finding a position for the servos which will allow operation of both ailerons and flaps will present some difficulty.

The spars taper slightly at the tip and some care will be required to keep them accurate. Making both spars at the same time by temporarily laminating together them is highly recommended.

DEGREE OF DIFFICULTY:

Our rating of '3' for this plan assumes some past experience with plans building. In some areas of the construction, the builder will need some ingenuity to arrange items which are not shown. Makes an excellent model of what has become a classic in every sense of the word.

1/4 SCALE

PIETENPOL 'SKY SCOUT'

FROM: Hangar One Hobby, 1402 Madison Ave., Montgomery, AL, 36107

SPAN: 81" DOD: 2 CHORD: 15" AREA: 1211 Sq. In.

LENGTH: 48.5" WEIGHT: 11-12 # ENGINE: .60-1.2

HISTORICAL:

Our earliest reference to the Pietenpol 'Sky Scout' is found in a magazine published in 1933. Full-scale drawings for the aircraft were offered for $5.00 and the instruction manual that went with them detailed how to convert the Ford Model T engine to aircraft use! Later versions of the "Pete" were "updated" to use the Model A Ford engine as a power plant.

The Sky Scout was the single seat version of the two-place 'Air Camper'; both of which were designed by B.H. Pietenpol. Wing span of the 'Scout was 27' 3", the wing chord was 60" and it was 16' 3" long. The airfoil was one designed by Bernie Pietenpol. It resembles a Clark 'Y' with a bit of undercamber between the two wing spars. An identification feature of the "Pete" were its outsized wheels; 26" diameter wheels were specified (and necessary for flights from the grass fields and farm meadows of the 30's).

Performance-wise, the Sky Scout **wasn't** a "barn-burner". High speed was noted as 62 mph and normal cruise was 55! The bird landed at 35 mph, within 250 feet. It took all of 150 feet for its takeoff run, and had an initial climb rate of 200 feet per minute.

Several "Petes" are still flying, both originals and of recent construction. Of course, most of the modern versions are updated as far as power plants are concerned. Many sport Corvair and Volkswagen "iron" up front.

PLAN:

This single large sheet plan details the construction of a "between the wars" homebuilt. The Pietenpol Sky Scout is less well known than its companion, the Pietenpol Air Camper, although they are very similar. The model is full quarter scale, but, at 81 inch span, it is more readily portable than most such large scale models.

Fuselage construction is standard model style. Most of the fuselage members are specified as hard 1/4 square balsa. As the fuselage is square except on top, only seven formers are required. Little pattern making and parts cutting is required for its construction. The cabane and main landing gear strut are mounted permanently inside the upper fuselage so must be in place before the upper deck is completed. A fiberglass cowling is available from Fiberglass Master.

Tail members are conventional construction and should provide no difficulty at all. These are wire braced. Proctor #108 anchors and Proctor turnbuckles are recommended for the external bracing for the tail group members.

Landing gear and cabane strut wires are clearly shown on the plan and making them will not be difficult as they are all quite straightforward in shape. A good solid bender will be required to bend the 1/4 inch music wire used for the main landing gear, however.

Construction of the wing is also very conventional in style. It is built in one piece on the building board. No dihedral is required, so no fussy alignment and joining will be needed. The wing is constant chord so a minimum of wing rib patterns is required. Including the tip rib, there are only five different ribs to be made. The wing struts are apparently functional so should be made up and mounted as specified. Both front and rear spars are 3/8 X 1 inch spruce. They should be quite strong enough to withstand any aerobatics of which the model is capable.

The "Pete" was powered with a Model "T" four cylinder engine, complete with radiator. These are detailed on the plan sheets and would certainly add to the realism of the model if they were made up and installed. The aft center section of the wing may be hinged out of the way to permit pilot access to the cockpit as was the case with the original. Instrument panel details are shown on the plan and duplication of the panel will also add to the scale appearance. Instrument faces should all be of WWI vintage, of course.

The prototype model was flown on an Enya 1.2 four stroke engine and this would be more than adequate. The use of a four stroke engine, rather than a two stroke .60 would also add to realism in flight.

The Sky Scout should be an easy model to campaign in a scale contest. It would not be difficult to do an excellent job on readying it for such competition, despite the fact that judges seem to prefer WWII fighters to homebuilts. However, properly detailed, and prototypically flown, the Pietenpol could do well in scale.

DEGREE OF DIFFICULTY:

This model is not a difficult construction project. Almost anyone with some building experience should be able to build and fly it with no problems. The structure is simple throughout; there just aren't any areas to cause problems. Our rating of 2 indicates a good starting place for plans building. The model should be a stable and gentle flyer as well.

1/4 SCALE

SPIRIT OF ST. LOUIS (RYAN-NYP)

FROM: Granada Services, 13214 Ingres Ave., Granada Hills, California. 91344

SPAN: 126" **CHORD: 21"** **DOD: 3** **AREA: 2640 Sq. In.**

LENGTH: 72 1/2" **WEIGHT: Unspecified** **ENGINE: Quadra 35**

HISTORICAL:

Lindbergh's modified Ryan M-1 hardly needs an introduction to anyone who knows anything at all about airplanes. The M-1 was a two-place cabin monoplane mail plane. The Spirit of St. Louis (which was named after the home of Lindbergh's sponsors for the trans-Atlantic flight) was a highly-modified single place version of the earlier Ryans. Its "cabin space" was filled with fuel tanks, giving the airplane a range of over 4,000 miles.

Span of the 'Spirit was 46 feet, with a fuselage 27 feet 5 inches long. Powered with a Wright J5-C engine of 237 HP. it was capable of a top speed of 124 MPH, fully loaded with 450 gallons of fuel.

The airplane was built to Lindbergh's order in 60 days. For his Paris flight, it is said that Lindbergh decided to omit a parachute and a radio, the latter because, "they cut out when you need them most." Forward visibility in the 'Spirit' was nil as the fuselage fuel tanks were in the way. Lindbergh's only visibility forward was through a periscope and was severely restricted.

On May 20th, 1927, Lindberg took off from Roosevelt Field, New York, and 33 1/2 hours later landed the Ryan-NYP (New York-Paris) in Paris, having flown a distance of 3609 miles, non-stop. This epic feat was done by dead-reckoning navigation as he did not even carry a sextant. His landfall on arrival over southern Ireland was less than five miles off his plotted course, a remarkable feat even by today's standards. The Spirit now resides in the National Air and Space Museum in Washington, D.C. and a replica is flown regularly by the EAA.

PLAN:

John Pahlow's plan for this very large model is a gem. He must also be a believer in the 'KISS' principle as this plan is elegant in it's simplicity of design. The plan set consist of six sheets, three large and three about half-size.

The prototype model has set several distance records and would make an excellent candidate for such record attempts. Its fuel carrying capacity has not been determined (as far as the writer is aware) and distances greatly in excess of those already flown should be quite easily accomplished.

The fuselage is made of balsa strip stock, 1/2 X 3/4 inch for the top and bottom longerons and 1/4 inch square vertical and diagonal members. Fuselage cross members are 1/4 X 1/2 inch. Most fuselage joints are gussetted. Construction is very straight-forward and should be easily accomplished by almost anyone.

A landing gear blank is shown full size on one of the pattern sheets and will not be difficult to make. This is of 3/16 inch aluminium sheet and will require some accurate metal work to drill (and tap, in some cases) the holes required. The remainder of the landing gear/strut connections, and the shock absorbing strut will require some metal working skill and the proper tools as well.

The tail group is of conventional construction and, as the parts are all quite large, their fabrication will be quite an easy task. Pahlow's model used cable controls for rudder and elevator and details of the mechanism are shown on the plan.

Wing plan sheets are provided for both wing panels. These are built up as separate assemblies and attach individually to the cabin sides. The constant chord wings require a minimum of pattern making and the ribs can be produced by the 'stack' method.

The spars are all from 1/2 inch balsa, 1" by 1/2" forward and 11/16" by 1/2" to the rear. All spars are webbed, front and rear from root to tip. The spar which forms the trailing edge of the wing at the ailerons also runs from root to tip. The trailing edge part of the ribs (behind the aileron spar) are made up separately and glued to the rear of this spar. (1/2 X 1 3/8") While the wing has significant strength on it's own, the struts are working struts and are required for flight, of course.

Generous use of gussets is made in the wing structure and they will add significant strength to the structure when properly applied.

Servos are shown at each aileron, which will require very long servo leads. Any radio using long leads should be checked to assure that it is not sensitive to any re-radiated signal propagated by the servo leads. Chokes or Ace Noise Traps may be used if there is an interference problem. Care must also be taken to assure the servo leads are made from wire of adequate size in order to avoid any severe voltage drop due to the resistance in the wire itself. These are large ailerons, so servos of adequate power are required here.

Mounting the servos at the aileron location provides a number of advantages as the linkage is short. The loss of movement is held to a minimum due to the short linkage and, as it is a simple connection. Access panels are shown in order to be able to service the servos if required.

DEGREE OF DIFFICULTY:

Plenty of construction (and material) in this one. No real complications with the possible exception of making the landing gear/strut structure. Even these should not tax the competent modeler. Our '3' suggest any experienced builder could produce a flyable 'Spirit from this plan.

1/4 SCALE

CLIPPED-WING TAYLORCRAFT

FROM: RCM Plans Service, 120 W Sierra Madre Blvd., Sierra Madre. Ca. 91024

SPAN: 88" CHORD: 16" DOD: 3 AREA: 1386 Sq. In.

LENGTH: 65 1/4" WEIGHT: 16- 20 # ENGINE: .91 - 2.6 C.I.

HISTORICAL:

When Mssr. Piper and Taylor parted ways in the 30's, each established his own airplane company. True to the configuration of the 'Taylor Cub', both companies produced two-place, single engined, high wing monoplanes. The craft from Taylor were dubbed, of course, Taylorcraft.

The Taylorcraft Aviation Corp. remained in existence through 1979, although they were no longer building aircraft. The Clipped Wing version of the T'Craft was, like the Monocoupe, first produced by modifying existing airframes. It soon became an approved production variant, stressed for aerobatics. Power for T'Craft included many of the 'flat-fours' available in the 40's and 50's, including Lycoming and Continental engines.

Span of the clipped-wing variant was

29' 4" and the fuselage was 21' 4". Probably, the most 'visible' of the aerobatic T'Crafts was the one flown by Duane Cole (and the subject of the plan at hand).

PLAN:

This two sheet plan set comes with a reprint of the article published on the model in the October, 1979 RC Modeler. The model can be a little squirrely, so read the article (before flying) to learn of the designers problems with his first flight. No, Virginia, it did NOT fly 'right off the building board!'

On the right power and well balanced and properly trimmed, the T'Craft can be quite aerobatic and a delight for the experienced to fly. The novice builder should not have any real trouble in building the model, but flying it will take an experienced hand. Wing loading, at 20 pounds, comes out at over 33 ounces per square foot. Any heavier, and the model might get a little dicey.

Fuselage construction is usual model practice, making use of basswood upper and lower main longerons and 3/8 in. square balsa for the upright and diagonal members. Fuselage outline (when covered) is maintained by 3/16 inch square basswood stringers.

No joint gussets are shown in the fuselage although a significant increase in strength can be gained through using them.

The late (and un-lamented) 'Super Hustler' engine is shown, but any of the usual gasoline engines, of the appropriate size, may be used in its place.

A landing gear blank is bent from 6061-T6 aluminium and should not present any problems. Cross bracing between the gear legs is provided by 3/16 inch music wire, bent to the proper shape.

All tail feathers are 'built-up' using 3/8 inch balsa sheet for the various parts required. All but two small pieces are straight stock, so no great amount of pattern making or parts cutting is needed. Tail group parts are shown braced and this bracing should not be omitted.

Wing construction is a little out-of-the ordinary as aluminium tube spars are used. This will not be a problem if one of the cyanoacrylates is used to glue the ribs to the tubing. These spars are of different sizes, but the material for them should be readily available. Only one wing panel is shown, and it is suggested that the other be built upside down on the face of the plan. It usually works better if the plan is oiled and the other panel built on the back of the plan sheet.

The forward spar nests in an appropriate tube in the top of the cabin and a turnbuckle is used to hold the wings in place. (The rear and larger tube is cut off flush with the root rib.) The turnbuckle must be equipped with a jam-nut (as shown on the plans) to keep the turnbuckle from 'un-winding' in flight and allowing the wings some slack.

Both the 'stock' wing and the clipped version are shown on the plan, so it is 'builders choice' as to which of them is to be built. (Trim color lines for Duane Cole's Clipped version are shown on the plan sheets.)

The wing struts are functional, of course, and must be constructed as shown in order to provide the support required. These should always be fitted to the wing on the airplane as differences in construction can alter their length slightly.

Aileron servos are shown at each root rib, one each side. This is a good way to provide for adequate power for these large ailerons and the electrical connection needed is more easily made than having to 'fiddle' with a mechanical linkage each time the model is flown.

Ribs are all cap-stripped with 1/4 inch balsa and the leading edge area is sheeted with 1/8 inch balsa, top and bottom.

DEGREE OF DIFFICULTY:

This Taylorcraft model should be a good performer on the right engine. The writer has seen several perform and they can be a little hard to handle if the CG is not properly located. The model builder with some experience at plans building (and who has been on the 'sticks' for a while) could have an exciting airplane on his hands. Our '3' indicates this is not for the 'first-time' plans builder.

21% FULL-SIZE

WACO MODEL ARE

FROM: U.S. QUADRA, 1032 E. Manitowoc Ave., Oak Creek, Wisconsin. 53154

SPAN: 87 1/4" (U), 61" (L) CHORD: 15" (U) 10" (L) AREA: 1800 Sq. In.

LENGTH: 70" WEIGHT: 20 - 24 # DOD: 4 ENGINE: Quadra 35/ 50 cc.

HISTORICAL:

Of all the so-called 'Classic' airplanes from the Golden Age, this writer has an affection for the Waco biplanes, and a special fondness for the 'E' Model. Certainly among the nicest looking of the cabin Waco's, the ARE has slender, almost dainty, lines and yet was a hairy-chested he-man of an airplane. Capable of carrying four people and their gear at speeds of 200 MPH and more, the Waco was a close rival to the Beechcraft Staggerwing, its contemporary.

The Weaver Airplane Co. (Waco) made their first airplane, the Seven, in 1923 and never looked back until shortly after WWII. Their then-current Aristocraft was not doing at all well so they took their wartime profits and folded things up.

The Model 'ARE' appeared in 1939, only four were ever sold and only one of them survives. It was bought by The New York Daily News when new, and now rests quietly, fully restored, in a hangar in Oshkosh, Wisconsin. The owner, Mr. David Jameson, generously provided Dario Brisighella with the opportunity to measure and photograph the last Waco 'ARE' for this plan.

The lone 'ARE' model which has been preserved is a piece of aviation history frozen in time. Thankfully, people like Mr. Jameson still exist and have helped save such jewels for the enjoyment of those of us who like Classic airplanes. Thanks too, to Dario Brisighella for his work in turning out this excellent plan.

PLAN:

Brisighella does very fine work indeed and his plans may be the best available, no matter what the subject. This three-sheet plan for the Waco ARE is no exception. Once opened, the need to peruse it carefully is felt by almost everyone who sees it. The detail on the plan sheets is generous without being overpowering. It provides everything the builder needs to know to construct a true scale model of this classic biplane.

Construction follows the usual model building practices, but is extremely well executed. Several small metal parts will need to be fabricated, but this should create no problems for the skilled plans builder.

Fuselage construction is simplified by shading the main structural members, making it easy to pick them out. Medium hard balsa is called for and the main longerons are laminated on the outer edges with balsa strips, making a very strong structural member. The major fuselage joints show plywood gussets in place.

Basic shape of the fuselage is circular back to the front edge of the cabin, then rather slab-sided aft. A minimum of formers is required although there are a considerable number of shaped parts which will have to be made. The transition between the rounded and flat areas takes place over a short distance, so some care will be required to get everything in the correct position and then, keep everything true.

The landing gear patterns are shown full size and the bracing wires between the gear legs are spring loaded inside the fuselage. An excellent way to provide for some 'give' in the occasional (and inevitable) hard landing. The landing gear assembly is available ready to use; ordering instructions on the plan.

The tail group is all framed up although with some differences from usual model building practice. The stab is cut from sheet stock. The original airplane had a plywood covered fin and stab while the control surfaces were fabric covered. The elevator outer edge areas project ahead of the hinge line for dynamic balance and these may carry weights to provide for static balance as well.

No engine is shown mounted, though the bolt pattern for the Quadra die cast mount is shown on the firewall pattern.

Both wings are of constant chord, but the upper is much wider. The upper wing has both ailerons and flaps; the lower, neither. Aileron and flap servos are shown mounted near the control surface location. Only half of each wing panel is shown on the plan sheet, so it will be necessary to construct the other (left) wing panel on the back of the plan.

The ailerons and flaps are hinged at the scale location using large Robart round hinge pins. These are mounted in tubing at the trailing edges of the fixed surfaces in order to extend the hinge location to the scale position.

Interplane strut mounts are an integral part of the wing and the struts are bolted in place. A very strong and dependable method of mounting them is shown on the drawing.

Many scale details are shown on the plan and reference is made to an article by Brisighella in the June 1981 issue of RC Modeler for additional detail on his method of moulding fiberglass parts in place on the model. It would be worth the builder's while to search out that article and use the method described to make some of the parts needed.

DEGREE OF DIFFICULTY:

While not a really difficult building task, to properly create a truly scale model as shown on the plan will require some painstaking work and dedication to the job. It would be a shame to do anything less with this excellent plan. Our '4' indicates a good deal of work will be required.

1/4 SCALE

WACO MODEL CTO

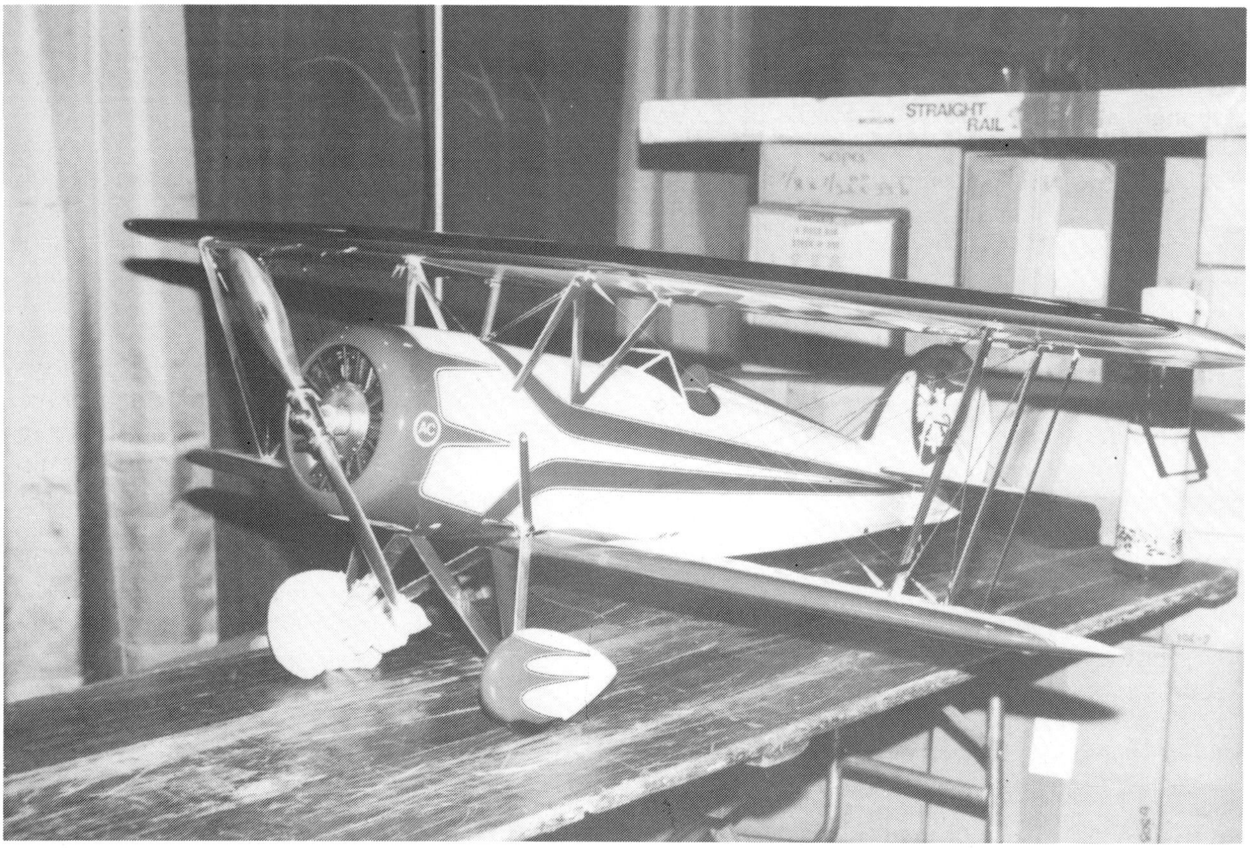

FROM: Model Builder Magazine, 621 W. 19th St. Costa Mesa, California. 92627

SPAN: 91" (U), 78" (L) CHORD: 15 5/8" (U), 10 1/2" (L) AREA: 1775 Sq. In.

LENGTH: 68" WEIGHT: Unspecified DOD: 3 ENGINE: 2 - 4 c.i.

HISTORICAL:

Another 'Classic' from the people at Waco. The 'Taperwing Waco' is easily recognized because of it's appearances in present-day air shows. This plan shows the Lyjak version which is both colorful and well documented.

Waco's (Wacko-not-Wayco) model identification system created a veritable monster. Almost every airplane built had a separate model designation. This CTO could have been ATO with an engine change. The first letter identifies the engine, (A= 330 HP Jacobs L-6MB, C= 250 HP Wright R-760). As there were 20 different engines used, you can almost take your pick.

As if that didn't make it difficult enough, the middle letter indicated which set of plans were used from which to build the airplane. Again, take your pick. The last letter designated the actual Model Number, but, there were exceptions. The three letter designators came into use after 1930, so anything built prior to that time didn't count. Confusing? Of course it was -- and it still is !

The Taperwing is built like a steel girder. Nobody ever broke one in the air and Bob Lyjak, whose airplane is the subject of this plan, is still flying his forty-five year old Taperwing at air shows trying diligently to do so without success. Strong hardly describes it. It could be called the Mack Truck of airplanes for strength and yet it can still perform with considerable agility.

PLAN:

This Model Builder plan by Larry Scott is on three sheets and is accompanied by the article which originally appeared with it in the pages of Model Builder. The article serves as a builders guide to construction.

The plan is 'black-line' and is nicely done. Clear and easy to read, the structure is simple and construction is very straight-forward.

Stick material for the basic fuselage structure is specified as 1/4" sq. spruce. No gussets are shown and their addition is highly recommended. No diagonal braces are shown top or bottom and their addition would increase the rigidity of the basic airframe, along with cross-member gussets. The minor weight penalty is worth the significantly increased strength.

The landing gear is bent from 1/4 inch piano wire so a sturdy bender will be required for this work. Landing gear is faired with balsa after assembly.

The firewall is shown as 1/4 inch material and it would be well to increase this to at least 3/8 inch or even 1/2 inch, depending on the engine used.

Empennage parts are all made up on 1/8 inch sheet stock overlaid with 1/8 inch square simulated ribs. This is a strong method of making these parts, but some care should be taken to use fairly light material in order not to create a tail heavy model. The weight of the engine chosen could minimize the danger of building 'tail heavy'. A heavy, powerful "hummer" can compensate for excess aft-end weight!

The stabilizer has been designed to provide adjustable incidence. This is a rather handy feature as it permits quite fine adjustment for trimming the airplane for proper flight. While this adjustment may only be used once, it is worth adding during construction. (An engine change, or any other major change in the model later, will also make good use of the adjustment.)

Wing construction is usual model practice and has been well thought out. The rib spacing appears to follow scale very closely and the wing, built as detailed on the plan, will be very strong. Front spars are 1/4 square, rear spars are 1/4 X 1/8 inch. Both sets of spars in both wings are plywood webbed part way to the tip. Roughly 2/3 and 1/3 of the span front and rear respectively.

The wings are both tapered, so a number of different wing rib patterns will be required. The designer has used the same ribs in both the upper and lower wings so they can be made up four at a time, in sets. The upper wing has two extra ribs, due to it's greater length. Only half of each wing is shown on the plan, so the other half must be built on the back of an oiled plan sheet. Wing panels are permanently joined after construction of the halves.

No aileron servo location is shown and standard practice would place them in the lower wing. Two servos should be used, one for each side of the airplane, as four ailerons could be a considerable load on a single servo. Servos may be installed near the aileron location or at the wing's center section. The center section could prove the better choice in this instance, as the wings begin to get rather thin at the aileron location.

Wing structure is very well designed as the trailing edge of the ribs is slotted to take a section of balsa 3/32 X 2 inches. Leading edge is 3/8 square balsa and 3/32 X 2 inch sheeting is used behind the leading edge. All ribs are cap-stripped.

DEGREE OF DIFFICULTY:

Nothing here of any great difficulty. The builder with some experience will have no trouble building the Waco and, even the newcomer to plans building should be able to get through this if he has a few kits under his belt. Nice looking, good flying, and potentially, a good scale subject. Thus our 3 out of 5.

1/4 SCALE

WACO HKS-7

FROM: Norm Rosenstock, 124 Granada St., Royal Palm Beach, Florida, 33411.

SPAN: 99 3/4" (U), 84 3/4" (L) CHORD: 14 1/4" (U) AREA: 2629 Sq. In.

LENGTH: 75 3/4" WEIGHT: 25 - 32 # DOD: 3 ENGINE: 2 -4 c.i.

HISTORICAL:

As we have mentioned previously, in relation to the Waco airplanes, almost every airplane built had a distinctive Model designation. Without going into the complications of Waco's system of identifying each model, the YKS-7 was the seventh improvement on the 'Standard Cabin Model' of the late thirties and early forties.

It was a four place airplane and the designator 'Y' indicates a 225 HP Jacobs radial engine (L-4MB). The 'K' identifies the factory plan set from which the airplane was built and the 'S' indicates a standard, four place cabin model. The number following the letter designators shows this was the seventh in a series of refinements and modifications to the original YKS airplane.

The model had a distinctive 'hump' over the upper wing and does not have the sleek lines of the later ARE/SRE models. Wing chord is the same in both wings, not true of the ARE/SRE.

The upper wing was fitted with both flaps and ailerons and four ailerons were standard. Fixed gear with faired gear legs were standard and some models were equipped with wheel pants.

Many Waco models exist in restored condition and much good documentation exists on them. The National Air and Space Museum has a library of 35,000 Waco photos!

PLAN:

This two sheet set, plus builder's manual, from Rosenstock is up to his usual good standard. Rosenstock has been around the modeling scene for a considerable number of years and is a skilled and knowledgeable draftsman.

A fiberglass cowling and wheel pants are available for the YKS; ordering details are on the plan sheets.

Construction throughout is standard model practice. The experienced will have no difficulty creating a good looking flyable model from the information supplied.

Framing material for the basic fuselage is spruce and the assembly is well gussetted at the joints, a feature of Rosenstock's plans which adds considerable strength to the structure.

While no engine is shown, the designer suggests that, if a smaller (2 c.i.) engine is to be used, the builder make an effort to keep the weight down to about 26-28 pounds. He also suggests some ways of doing this. If a larger engine is chosen, the model will fly well at 32 pounds, with a wing loading of approximately 27 ounces per square foot. This wing loading is very favorable and the model should fly well, with adequate power, even at the upper end of the weight specified.

Landing gear parts are 1/4 inch piano wire which will require the use of a sturdy bending machine. The shapes are not particularly complicated and should not be a problem.

Tail group members are conventional stick construction. The outer ends of the elevator project forward beyond the hinge line and the adding of weight in this area will static balance the elevators. This is an excellent idea and can reduce the load on the elevator servo. Control of each half of the elevator is independent and, although the plan shows a 'Y' control link attached to both halves, it would not be a problem to use two servos for elevator control.

The building manual suggests that the tail group bracing wires are necessary to flight and the model should not be flown without them. Omission of these important braces will almost certainly lead to disaster during flight.

Wing construction is also standard model practice and should not provide any great difficulty to the experienced. Wing spar material is not specified but the spars are quite large. Front spars are 1/4 X 1 inch and the rear spars are 1/4 X 3/4 inch in both wings. Ribs are made to slide down over the spars, leaving the area between the spars 'empty'. This void area is subsequently filled with inserted bracing pieces following completion of the basic wing structure.

Wing to fuselage mounting is by way of aluminium spar joiners assembled through the fuselage which project into box spars in each wing panel. Bolts are then threaded into blind nuts (from below) through the aluminium spar joiner and box spar receiver to retain the wings in place. This certainly has every appearance of being more than adequate.

An aileron servo is shown in each lower wing panel and, while outboard of the root rib, they are inboard of the aileron location. A conventional solid aileron link, bellcrank and pushrod are used to drive the ailerons.

The wing struts and 'N' struts are required for flight and the manual goes into some detail as to the the making of the struts and the fitting of them in place. This latter is important as it is also setting up the wing incidence and wing spacing for accuracy before the struts are fitted.

DEGREE OF DIFFICULTY:

While generally of conventional construction, this is not a model with which to learn to build from plans. Our three indicates the beginner should start somewhere else. Good flying and fine looking biplane with the capability of entering scale contests.

1/4 SCALE

WATERMAN AEROBILE

FROM: Mammoth Scale Plans, 3351 Pruneridge Ave., Santa Clara CA. 95051

SPAN: 91" CHORD: 16.5" AREA: 1804 Sq.In.

LENGTH: 48.5" WEIGHT: 22# DOD: 3 ENGINE: 2-4 C.I.

HISTORICAL:

This highly unusual airplane was developed by Waldo Waterman in 1935 to compete in the Vidal Safety Airplane Competition. Waldo obviously had some good ideas as the Aerobile was a co-winner of that competition.

There were six Aerobiles built in 1936 and 37. Five of these were powered with (of all things!) a Studebaker auto engine of 100 horse power. The engine was liquid cooled and the radiator was situated immediately behind the opening in the nose. The sixth example had a Tucker auto engine installed and that airplane now resides in the San Diego Aerospace Museum.

These novel and practical airplanes were easy to fly, stall proof, and should carry these qualities over into a model. The scale airfoil (NACA 23012) used in the original is duplicated in this large and impressive model. This is a semi-symetrical airfoil and was also used in the Beechcraft Staggerwing. While the airplane is anything but conventional in shape, the methods used in construction of the model are quite conventional.

PLAN:

The plan consists of two sheets, one large sheet and one of average size. While the airplane is unconventional in shape, construction follows standard model practice and is detailed on the plan for ease of construction. The forward cabin sides are made in two sections and these are then assembled into the finished fuselage. Step-by-step instructions for this work are noted on the plan. As the engine is mounted in the pusher position behind the cabin, there is a cooling air duct running through the fuselage which will also serves as a stiffener and support for the cabin assembly.

The forward cabin support braces are fabricated from brazing rod and are brazed together to form the support assembly. Several formers are required, some fairly large, but none of these should be difficult to pattern or to make up. While the cabin assembly may look a little tricky, it should not prove difficult if proper care is taken to maintain the correct shape. This work may be done over the plan and the cooling air duct will assist in keeping everything properly aligned. The Zenoah 2.2 c.i engine is shown installed and should be more than adequate for the model at the weight specified. The CG is shown just aft of the cabin and a few inches forward of the engine. Checking the balance of the model during construction will assure that no serious out-of-balance problems develop.

The landing gear is quite simple and can be made from 3/16" music wire for the nose gear and 1/4" wire for the mains. There is a minimum amount of spring in the main gear which mounts to the aft bottom fuselage. The airplane sits very close to the ground due to the excellent ground clearance provided the propeller by the rear mounted engine. Breaking a prop on this model would be difficult!

Wing construction is quite conventional with the exception that the wings are raked aft at the tip. The short center section is not raked but is square to the fuselage. As the wings are constant chord, only a minimum number of rib patterns are required. Control runs for rudder and ailerons are in the wing as the rudders are mounted at each wing tip. These make use of C.B. Associates pulleys and International RC Specialties cable. (Address on plan sheet.) The control runs must be set up carefully before covering, of course.

There is substantial washout in this wing and a pattern for a washout jig is shown on the drawing. This washout IS NECESSARY for the model to fly properly. The wing struts are not required for flight and simply plug into place for scale appearance.

Fin and rudder construction is quite standard and is detailed on the plan. There is no elevator so the ailerons are actually elevons and the mixing function may be done from the transmitter, if available, or mechanically within the model. Both methods are shown. The rudder movement is away from the wingtip only, and an ingenious method of permitting one rudder to move at a time from a single servo is utilized.

DEGREE OF DIFFICULTY:

While unconventional in shape, this model should not prove overly difficult to build. Some care and attention during construction will be necessary as there are some unusual conditions to be provided for. Our 3 indicates a moderately difficult model which should fly very well.

1/4 SCALE

GEE BEE R-1 SUPER SPORTSTER

FROM: Henry Haffke, 1038 W. Elmer St., Vineland N.J. 08360

SPAN: 75" **CHORD: 12" (Avg.)** **AREA: 900 Sq. In. (Apprx.)**

LENGTH: 52" **WEIGHT: 14-15#** **DOD: 4** **ENGINE: .91**

HISTORICAL:

The Granville Brothers (GB) of Springfield, Massachusetts were, collectively, aeronautical geniuses. Their racers exemplified the Golden Age of air racing and their "pinnacle" was their model R-1, which won the Thompson Trophy in 1932. With a snarling Pratt & Whitney Wasp up front and Jimmy Doolitle at the controls, the R-1 set a new speed record for the Thompson and the world -- 296 mph!

Although the barrel-shaped racer **looked** different, it was, aerodynamically, rather simple. From a construction viewpoint, it was early 30's state-of-the-art. The 17' 9" fuselage was steel tubing, with fairing and stringers continuing the circular cross-section (max. diameter: 61") from the engine to the tapered vestigal fin and rudder. The aft-mounted cockpit suspended the pilot amongst the spidery steel work. The wings were wood (25' span) and held the widely spaced landing gear. Every effort was made to "streamline" the aircraft.

The aft fuselage, wings and tail feathers were fabric covered. The R-1 weighed 1840 lbs. empty and had a max. gross of 3075 with full fuel tanks. Its sister-ship, the R-2 was designed as a cross-country racer and had a different engine (Wasp Jr.) and larger fuel tanks. Except for markings, the R-2 differed externally from the pylon-polishing R-1 primarily in the shape of the cowling. These differences are readily apparent on the Bill Hannan drawings for the R-1/R-2 contained in the Williams Bros. plastic kit for the Gee Bee. It's a good place to begin "documenting" your Gee Bee R-1 model.

PLAN:

Henry Haffke is probably the world's greatest expert on the Granville Brothers' airplanes. The Gee Bee series of racing and sport airplanes have endured a great deal of adverse comment, and, according to Henry, very much undeserved. He has modeled almost all of the airplanes built by the Granvilles (And is probably working on the remainder!) They fly well and Henry has won several trophies with them.

Despite its rather unusual shape, the Gee Bee R-1 is not difficult to build. Very conventional structures and methods are used throughout; it's just bigger. Henry suggests keeping lightness in mind during construction and, with the Webra .91 on which the prototype was flown, that's probably sound advice.

The plan consists of four medium sized sheets. Two of these are almost entirely patterns for the multitude of parts required. A good deal of time will be required to transfer all the patterns to building material before construction can begin. Some of the parts (especially the cowling) are quite large although they can better be drawn with a beam compass than traced.

The fuselage box sides are framed over the plan as usual. The fuselage shape is formed through the use of formers and stringers. There are a total of 40 formers to make and 37 stringers will be mounted on them. Obviously this is work which will require some patience and attention to detail to complete properly. The after end of the Gee Bee is fabric covered, so any lack of precision in placing the stringers will show through the covering material.

The stabilizer is made from 1/4 inch sheet stock. The elevator is also sheet stock with light ribs mounted on both sides. The vertical fin is built up (although there isn't much to build) and the rudder is built up from sheet stock and external ribs as is the elevator. A novel method of hinging is used and the parts required are shown clearly on the plan.

The landing gear is bent from 3/16 inch wire. This doesn't tell half the story as the landing gear fairings and wheel pants will take a lot of work. None of this is difficult however, and its proper completion will add significantly to the good appearance of the model.

Wing construction is again quite conventional. The rear spar requires some shaping toward the tip, but nothing to cause alarm. Unfortunately, only one wing panel is shown and it will either be necessary to have a reverse copy made or oil the plan and work from the backside. While this is not as convenient as having both panels on the plan sheet, by building the first panel from the front of the plan, the panel done on the reverse of the plan won't be too difficult.

Aileron operation is by 1/4 inch aluminum torque rod. Be sure the material used for this torque tube is fairly stiff and does not twist out of shape when force is applied.

While the wing is not exactly constant chord, it doesn't taper all that much so a minimum of wing rib patterns are required; seven in total. Various bracing wires were used on the original, but are not required on the model other than for accuracy of detail. Much good documentation exists for this famous airplane (See Documentation section) and it would not be difficult to properly detail it for competition if desired.

DEGREE OF DIFFICULTY:

Definitely not for the beginner. Some experience should be gained before staring such an ambitious project. Depending on the power installed, it could be a hot airplane. Thus our rating of 4.

NOTE: Henry, in conversation with the authors, states that the power specified for his 1/4-scale Gee Bees (usually a .90 two-stroke or its four-cycle equivalent) is **plenty** of engine. He doesn't recommend over-powering his designs.

WEDELL-WILLIAMS GILMORE RED LION

FROM: Wendell Hostetler, 1041 Heatherwood Lane, Orrville, Ohio, 44667

SPAN: 84" CHORD: 15" AREA: 1200 Sq. In.

LENGTH: 67" WEIGHT: 19-22 POUNDS DOD: 4 ENGINE: 2-5 HP

HISTORICAL:

Our "cover girl", Roscoe Turner's Gilmore Red Lion Wedell-Williams racer had a long and successful career. Built in 1932, Roscoe won the 1934 Thompson Trophy (but **not** with the Gilmore paint job) after twice changing engines to increase the bird's horsepower. Colonel Turner also used the Wedell-Williams in Bendix Trophy races. He, finally, came to grief when he cracked up in New Mexico enroute to the 1936 Bendix starting point. Matty Laird was called on to rebuild the racer and in the process, increased the diameter of the forward fuselage by an imperceptible 3". The aircraft still exists and at this writing is being rebuilt in Texas.

NR-61Y spanned 26 feet and was 20' 11" long. With its ultimate 1690 cu. in. Hornet power plant, its Thompson Trophy-winning speed was 248.13 mph. The racer was capable of higher, straight-out speeds and was timed at 295.47 mph in the

1934 Shell Speed Dashes.

PLAN:

Another of Wendell Hostetler's Classic racers from the 1930's. As is to be expected from this experienced designer, the Gilmore Red Lion is an excellent plan which can produce a fine looking and good flying model. Wendell's own prototype shows what a fine job can be done from one of his plans.

The set consists of two sheets of drawings which are well done and well spaced on the sheets. Wendell's plans have a professional look and are uncluttered and easy to read. Everything needed by the experienced builder is present on the plan sheets. While very complete, this is not a plan recommended for the beginner at plans building. As a racer, and depending on the engine installed, the Red Lion is apt to be a fairly "hot" performer as well.

The fuselage sides, of stick construction, are sheeted with 3/16 balsa through their entire length and both a 1/4" balsa and a 1/16" plywood doubler are used on the forward section. This construction will provide the strength and rigidity required on the long fuselage. The engine mounts quite a distance forward of the main part of the fuselage and the weight of the engine so far foward will require the strength built into the structure as shown.

A considerable number of formers are shown, requiring quite a lot of pattern making and parts cutting to provide the shape to the fuselage. 40 stringers are placed in these formers to hold the shape of the covering material. The fuselage is balsa sheeted from the firewall to the cockpit so the stringers do not run the full length of the fuselage. The firewall is noted as two pieces of 1/4 plywood laminated together, although this could be a single piece of good quality standard plywood and still be adequate to the job.

The fuel tank is shown mounted across the fuselage and this could lead to problems with fuel feed, depending on the engine used. It would be as well to mount the tank parallel to the center line of the fuselage if possible. (It is not apparent why this was done.) An upper fuselage hatch and the wing mounting opening give good access to the interior of the fuselage.

Several accessory parts are available. The cowling, the nose piece, wheel pants and landing gear fairings are all available in fiberglass from T & D Fiberglass Specialties, and the heat treated, shock mounted landing gear are available from Bob Shattleroe. The engine shown on the plan is the 3.1 c.i. Sachs-Dolmar.

All tail members are constructed from 3/8" balsa sheet, so require no more than the transfer of patterns to the sheeting and then shaping them. Both the model prototype and true scale outlines are shown.

The wing is built in three sections with the outboard sections being held in place with machine screws through the central box spar. The outer section spars extend into the box spar right to the center line of the fuselage and appear to have more than adequate strength for the loads which may be applied. Scale flying wires may be added if desired although the designer indicates they are not necessary for flight. The landing gear is attached to a 3/8" plywood plate in the wing so the model will sit on its gear with the center section in place.

While the wing is not entirely constant chord, only four ribs of different lengths are required for each wing. The bulk of the wing ribs are the same size. The model prototype has slightly longer than scale wings and the degree of shortening required for true scale is shown on the plan. Aileron servo location is shown at the aileron, so longer than normal servo leads will be required. If there is any doubt, the radio equipment should be checked to assure there is no "feedback" from these long servo leads. Alternatively, Ace filters or some other means of eliminating this feedback should be used.

The markings on the airplane are numerous and some will require considerable skill with a paint brush. So far as is known, no appropriate decal set is available. However, all markings are shown on the plans sheets.

DEGREE OF DIFFICULTY:

The Red Lion makes an excellent scale subject and should make a good flying subject, keeping in mind the markings will require some skill and care. Not for the rank beginner. Fairly conventional construction but lots of it. We ranks Hostetler's Wedell-Williams Racer as a '4' on our scale of 5.

1/5 SCALE

FRANK HAWKS' TIME FLIES

FROM: Henry Haffke, 1038 W. Elmer Rd., Vineland, N.J. 08360

SPAN: 72" **CHORD: 16.5" (Root) 9" (Tip)** **AREA: 918 Sq.In.**

LENGTH: 52" **WEIGHT: Unknown** **DOD: 3** **ENGINE:. 90 C.I.**

HISTORICAL:

Frank Hawks was a record-setter in the 30's. His ultimate mount was "Time Flys", designed by Howell Miller and built by craftsman from the Granville Brothers organization. The aircraft was sponsored by the Gruen Watch Co.; hence the aircraft's name.

Powered by a P&W R-1830 BG of 1150 HP, Time Flys was capable of cruising at 340 mph (max. speed 375) for cross-country record attempts. The fuselage was built on a steel tubing frame and covered with Haskelite plywood. The plywood covered wing (31' span) had three internal spars. The tail surfaces were steel tube outlines with spruce spars and plywood ribs.

The craft was equipped with a retractable landing gear. The most unusual feature of the bird was the windshield/cockpit seat arrangement. For take off and landing, the seat was cranked up 12" and the streamlined, transparent "cockpit cover" became the **windshield**!

Hawks had a lot of problems with Time F-lys and his last accident cracked the main wing spar. The aircraft languished for years in a hangar until it was reincarnated as the MAC-1 by the Military Aircraft Corp., and modified as a tandem two-seater for an Army fighter competition. In this configuration, it was flown by Leigh Wade in the 1938 Thompson Trophy race, placing 4th with a speed of 248.42 mph.

PLAN:

Another of Henry Haffke's Classic racing airplanes from the Golden Age of Air Racing. Time Flies has distinctive lines and is typical of the racing monoplanes of the 30's. It looks like an engine with an airplane screwed on behind it! Most of the 30's racers had a similar appearance, almost as if the airplane was an afterthought to the provision of an engine. Two plan sheets provide only minimal printed detail, so some experience in plans building is indicated as required.

Fuselage construction here is a little out of the ordinary. The formers are assembled to an upper and a lower quarter square keel. There is a doubler over the wing saddle area, but the keel method of construction will require some care and attention to "get it right" the first time. The easiest way to do this is to pin the keels down on the plan sheets, then assemble one set of side formers to the keels. The doubler should be added while the assembly is still pinned down. Then comes the hard part. After the glue is properly dry (a good place to use Hot Stuff or one of the other CA's) the assembly is removed from the board and the formers for the other side are then assembled in place. (an even better place to use Hot Stuff!) No fuselage top view is shown on the plans.

An alternative which will assure the alignment does not change while handling the structure is to apply the 1/8 inch sheeting while the first side is still pinned to the building board. The entire fuselage us sheeted with 1/8 planking and once in place, the completed side will be pretty firm. Then adding the formers for the opposite side and planking them will complete the fuselage. If you have not planked before, do not use strips of planking that are too wide. While it does take longer to add a number of slender planks than wide ones, a much better job is realized and not so much of the skin has to be sanded away to provide a pleasing contour to the finished product. Keep in mind that the lower fuselage section beneath the wing is part of the wing and not part of the fuselage.

The windshield in the original airplane was retractable and a pair of small windows were provided in the sides of the cockpit to provide the pilot with at least a semblance of an outside view. This windshield could be made retractable in the model to add additional realism.

Landing gear parts are shaped piano wire and full sized patterns are shown. These are made from 5/32 wire and the usual bender should be adequate to form them. There are a few shapes which are slightly complex so some care will need to be exercised to get them right. Time Flies had a rather complex landing gear strut arrangement which provided "knee action" shock absorbing. This mechanism is shown, along with the fairings which cover it. Here again, some care and attention to detail will be required to duplicate the original in miniature.

Wing construction is conventional although only the left wing panel is shown. As with many Haffke designs, the aileron is operated through the use of a torque tube called out as aluminum. This should be a tubing of adequate rigidity to prevent it twisting out of shape and reducing the aileron movement. Time Flies has a double tapered wing so each wing rib is distinct in shape. Ten patterns are required.

The dihedral braces are inserted through slots in the wing ribs so are not glued to the spars. For this reason, the dihedral braces are quite a bit longer than usual. Six pieces of 1/4 square are used inboard of the aileron as additional transverse members at the surface of the rib. Four are used outboard of the inner edge of the aileron. This gives the appearance of providing quite adequate wing strength.

DEGREE OF DIFFICULTY:

Our 3 indicates that this is not a plan for the raw beginner and that the structure will require some skill and care to construct a flyable model from it. Not a great deal of detail is shown on the plan and some experience will provide the information which is not shown.

1/4 SCALE

TURNER SPECIAL LTR-14

FROM: Wendell Hostetler, 1041 Heatherwood Lane, Orrville, Ohio. 44667

SPAN: 84" (75") CHORD: 16 3/4" (Root) 11 5/8 (Tip) AREA: 1275 Sq. In.

LENGTH:70" WEIGHT: 18 - 22 # DOD: 4 ENGINE: 2 - 5 H.P.

HISTORICAL:

Roscoe Turner's "ultimate" racing airplane, the Laird-Turner LTR-14 was built to his specifications. But, not without a considerable gestation period. As originally designed (and built) the craft had a constant chord wing with rounded tips. Engineering considerations soon revealed that the craft had an inadequate amount of wing area for its weight and intended speed. Roscoe, thus, turned the airplane over to Matty Laird who built the tapered wing that appears on the bird today, on display in the National Air & Space Museum in Washington, D.C.

Although Colonel Turner flew the aircraft in the 1937 National Air Races, a missed pylon denied him the Thompson Trophy. In 1938, with modifications to the oil cooling system and the addition of wheel pants, the LTR-14 was successful and gave Roscoe his second Thompson victory.

Like with his Wedell-Williams racer, Turner had several sponsors for the Turner Racer. Thus, model builders are cautioned to cross-check model configuration against markings for a specific racing year.

The LTR-14 spanned 25' 4"; was 24' 3" long and 10 feet high, overall. Its 1938 Thompson-winning speed was 293.419, a new record. Power was a P&W Twin Wasp, Senior of 1100 horsepower. It should be noted that Roscoe also won the 1939 Thompson in the LTR-14, but at a slightly slower speed.

PLAN:

Wendell Hostetler has produced several plans over the past few years. This one for the Turner Special Racer maintains the high standards he has set in the past with his other plans. Two plans sheets and a manual of instructions make up the set.

A fiberglass cowling, wheel pants, nose piece, air scoops and a spring loaded landing gear assembly are available; ordering details are on the plan.

Fuselage construction makes use of 3/16 balsa sheet sides, reinforced with 1/4 square balsa strips inside. The forward third of the fuselage is quite well strengthened with 1/4 inch sheet balsa between the 1/4 square members. This will provide excellent strength with an acceptable weight increase.

A considerable number of formers will be required due to the shape of the fuselage. Most of these are generously notched for the stringers, so a good deal of time will be spent making patterns and then producing the parts needed for construction.

The landing gear legs are made up from 1/4 inch piano wire, so a strong wire bending tool will be needed, or the available gear may be ordered instead. The available gear is spring loaded and will save considerable time and effort.

The engine shown is the Sachs-Dolmer 3.1 c.i. A comparable engine could be substituted, of course.

The vertical fin and rudder are conventional construction, requiring only a few cut parts. The stab and elevator are airfoil in shape and will require some care during assembly in order to produce a 'true' structure. The making of patterns and parts will take some time here before construction can begin.

A split elevator is shown, driven by separate elevator servos. This will provide some additional safety in the event of losing a servo; but only if the failed servo is in the neutral position. Airtronics 100 oz/in servos are recommended for all control surfaces. In such a potentially high speed model, this suggestion should be given serious consideration.

One panel each, of two different wings are shown on the plan. The longer (non-scale) wing will produce a model of lower speed and better wing loading than the shorter, scale-length wing. These span 84" and 75" respectively. Either may be fitted with no change in the fuselage structure. It would be possible to build both sizes of wings and produce a true scale model which could easily be converted to a slower flying model of lower wing loading.

The wing center section is built separate from the wings and may be removed from the fuselage as an assembly on it's own. Wings are mounted via spars 'nesting' into box spars in the fuselage.

Wing construction is conventional built up style. Since the Turner features a tapered wing, individual wing ribs will need to be patterned and cut. The rear spar is tapered, so an accurate job of measuring and cutting this spar will be necessary.

Aileron servo location is directly forward of the aileron so the radio gear being used must be checked to assure the longer than normal servo leads don't require chokes or Noise Traps.

DEGREE OF DIFFICULTY:

Definitely not for the beginning builder or flyer. While quite straight-forward in construction methods used, there is a good deal of work involved, much of it requiring patience and skill to complete. Our rating of '4' indicates this to be a model for the experienced builder and the capable model pilot.

1/5 SCALE

CURTISS P-40D (WARHAWK)

FROM: Nick Ziroli, 29 Edgar Drive, Smithtown, New York. 11787

SPAN: 94" CHORD: 22" Root, 10" Tip AREA: 1525 Sq.In.

LENGTH: 77" WEIGHT: 20 to 30# DOD: 4 ENGINE: 2 TO 4 c.i.

HISTORICAL:

The last of the real Hawks, the Curtiss P-40 series of aircraft were the logical successors to the all-metal, low-winged retractable landing gear design begun with the P-36, Model 75. In fact, aft of the firewall there were only subtle differences in construction and aerodynamic shape. It's easy to trace the Warhawk's pedigree through the YP-37 and the XP-42. Basically, the '40 was a '36 with an Allison liquid cooled engine replacing the Wright air cooled radial. In fact, the tenth P-36 was used to produce the first P-40 in just that fashion -- in 1937. Almost obsolete at the beginning of World War II, the US Warhawk (Tomahawk to the British) had two big advantages going for it. First, it was in serial production and therefore readily available. Second, the design was easily modified and updated with improved engines (the F-model's Packard-Merlin) and increased armament (the addition of six 50 cal. wing guns, replacing earlier 30 cal.

synchronized fuselage-mounted guns). Later P-40's, beginning with the L-model, featured extended fuselages and the "N" was a relatively pleasant model to fly. The ultimate '40 the "Q", had a bubble canopy and rivalled the performance of the P/F-51D.

The following specifications represent those applicable to the "short-fuselage models" of the P-40. Span: 37'4"; Length: 33'4"; Height: 12'4". The "F" (Merlin-engined) version had 1,300 hp available at 12,000 ft. and 1,120 hp available for takeoff; cruised at 290 mph with a 364 mph top speed and its 157 gallons of internal fuel gave it a range of 375 miles. Max gross weight was 9,350 lbs and the empty weight was 6,590. The 'D' Model P-40 came about as a result of the British adding four .50 caliber machine guns in the wings in place of the single .30 and single .50 caliber guns originally fitted on either side of the engine, firing through the propeller arc.

PLAN:

Nick Ziroli's plans show the mark of an experienced model builder. The plans are nicely drawn and well reproduced. Sharp, clear and readable. While no building booklet is provided, the copious notes on the plan, coupled with a series of construction photos included, leave little to be desired as far as building from the plan is concerned. The plan consists of four sheets, one of which is mainly patterns, thus avoiding cutting the main parts of the plan up. Cowling, canopy, and spinner are available.

Typical of Ziroli's plans, the fuselage is built on a 'crutch'. This makes the structure a little lighter than the conventional stick structure and also provides a resistance to the deforming of the fuselage under load. The crutch is particularly useful where the fuselage surface is a collection of compound curves as is the case with most WWII fighters. The crutch must be raised from the building board while the fuselage formers are assembled to it and it is important that the crutch's shape be maintained while this assembly is taking place.

The Quadra engine is shown, but at the heavier end of the weight specified, it may well be too small for good performance. In addition, a larger, heavier engine will provide useful (and necessary) nose weight. (The prototype required two pounds of lead in the nose to properly adjust the CG.)

The fuselage sub-structure is strip covered with 1/8" balsa sheet planking. If this work has not been attempted before, care should be taken to assure a good glue joint between the sheeting strips and the sub-structure. The temptation is to use wide strips in order to get the sheeting done quickly. This will produce a weak structure when the sheeting is sanded to it's finished form. Better to use many narrow (and close fitting) strips than fewer, wide ones.

Wing construction is quite straightforward with aileron servos mounted near the root rib. Trailing edge split flaps are indicated on the plan but may be omitted if not wanted. As can be expected with a tapered wing, many wing ribs are required so plenty of pattern making and parts cutting will be required. Ziroli shows a one half inch washout at the wing tip on the P-4O plan. This twist (leading edge downward) in the wing will go a long way towards preventing tip stalls at low speeds. Providing this washout takes a little time and patience; do not neglect it. Your P-4O will fly a great deal better with it than without. Keep in mind that adding a servo for each wing (and possibly one for each half of the elevator) will produce more than the usual battery drain. For this reason, a larger than 'normal' battery pack should be used as well as a redundant battery system. In addition, Noise Traps should be used if there is any doubt about your radio's ability to reject such interference.

Retracts are available which could be used in the P-4O, adding much to it's scale realism. However, as with the Corsair, these gear legs and wheels retract to the rear, transferring weight aft during retraction. This transfer of weight to the rear should be taken into account when the model is being balanced for proper CG location. Too much weight moved to the rear in flight can create a model which is difficult to control.

DEGREE OF DIFFICULTY:

While not overly difficult for the experienced builder, if building on a crutch is a new experience, some care should be taken to assure accuracy. The number of patterns required and the fuselage sheeting will tax the abilities of the inexperienced builder. Thus a 4 on our scale of five.

1/5th SCALE

DOUGLAS SKYRAIDER A1-H

FROM: Mammoth Scale Plans, 3351 Pruneridge Ave., Santa Clara, CA. 95051

SPAN: 120" CHORD: 26.3" (Root) 13" (Tip) AREA: 2321 Sq. In.

LENGTH:92" WEIGHT: 35 # DOD: 4 ENGINE: TA 51

HISTORICAL:

The Douglas Skyraider was the most widely used Navy attack aircraft in the immediate Post WW II period. Designed in 1944, the AD-1 was placed on order on April 18, 1945. Subsequent production and modification was substantial; the last variant was designated the AD-7.

The AD-1 was a B-I-G airplane. It spanned 50 feet; was 39' 5" long; 9 feet high and was powered by the Wright R-3350 engine of 2,500 takeoff horsepower. Its lifting ability was only limited by the number of "hard-points" installed in its huge wing. Its empty weight was 10,508 lbs. and max gross was a staggering 18,030 lbs. Maximum speed of the Skyraider is listed as 366 mph at 13,500 feet, while it cruised at 185. Landing speed was a reasonable 84 mph. The aircraft featured fuselage-mounted dive brakes.

The basic airframe/engine combination was modified as a single and two-place radar-equipped night fighter. The AD-5 version featured a larger rudder and a two-man crew. In this incarnation the aircraft could carry eight passengers or four litter patients!

PLAN:

This plan for the Douglas Skyraider is a monumental effort on the part of Bob Morse of Mammoth Scale Plans. The plan itself consists of three very large sheets and there is little of that surface which is not covered with detailed information on the construction of this very large model. Keep in mind that such a large model will require a large building surface. The fuselage is 95" long and each wing panel is 5 feet long. As they are mated on the building board, a ten foot building board would not be overly large. While the construction is not unduly difficult, there is a **VERY** great deal of it. This is not a model to be built in a hurry and it will require considerable attention to detail to complete it properly. **MINIMUM** engine size recommended is the Kawasaki TA 51 of 3.15 cubic inches. This model would not suffer from additional power, even up to 5 cubic inches. It would be difficult to overpower it. (The 3.15 engine suggested was among the most powerful available at the time the plan was drawn.)

The basic fuselage is a framed, stick, structure with each side built over the plan. While the material used (1/4 square) may seem rather light, there is considerable reinforcing applied as construction continues. All corners are gusseted. Due to the shape of the fuselage, a considerable number of formers will be required and they are cut from 1/4" sheet balsa. The entire fuselage is sheeted with 3/16" and 1/4" balsa, so a goodly supply of sheet stock should be on hand before construction begins.

The tail group is conventional construction, and, as with everything else, are quite sizable. The stab span is four feet, for example. The stab trailing edge and elevator leading edge are laminated so as to accommodate the hinges. All tail group members are sheeted.

A fixed landing gear is shown although both a fixed gear assembly or a custom retract system is available from Phil Karafilis. A cowling is available from Paul Steiner and a canopy can be ordered from Mammoth Scale Plans. All these addresses are shown on the plan.

Wing construction is rather complex, depending on the equipment installed. The flaps are shown as being operated by a Rhom Air retract system, and incorporate a Hydrolock mechanism. If both flaps and retracts are to be used (and what a shame if they were not) there is a good deal of hardware to be made up and installed inside the wing during construction. Both wing panels are shown and each has some of the details required.

Wing spars are 1/4 X 1/2 inch spruce, top and bottom and these are then webbed with vertical grain 3/32 sheet balsa. In effect, a very strong box spar is made in place within the wing after the ribs are in place. Some care is required in framing such a wing in order to keep all parts in their proper places accurately. Formidable strength is available in such a structure, properly built.

The wing is tapered and each wing panel requires sixteen ribs. These are large so a considerable quantity of sheet stock will be needed from which to make them. It will be very important to assure that all the mechanical items are installed in the wings during the appropriate stage of construction. There is included a short listing of the construction steps required and it would be as well to refer to them during construction in order to avoid any omissions. The flap operating linkage consists of a torque rod operated by a Rhom retract unit. (One unit operates both left and right flaps.) This Rhom unit is locked in intermediate positions by the Hydrolock unit, taking what could be high loads off the servo. Aileron movement is transmitted through a "pull-pull" double Nyrod linkage operated by a servo for each aileron. Servos for this purpose must be quite powerful to assure proper control.

DEGREE OF DIFFICULTY:

This model is not for the beginner. Considerable experience with plans building should be gained elsewhere before taking on such a project. There is a very large quantity of building to be done and some of it is painstaking work. If not properly and carefully built, the model could be a major disappointment. Nor is it going to be a large "baby-carriage" in the air. Good flying skills will be required to control it. A definite 4, leaning toward a '5'.

1/4 SCALE

FAIRCHILD PT-19

FROM: Taylorcraft, 216 Willow Ave., Roseville, Ca. 95678

SPAN: 108" **CHORD: 21 3/4" - 13 1/2"** **AREA: 1845 Sq. In.**

LENGTH: 81 1/2" **WEIGHT: 23 -33#** **DOD: 4** **ENGINE: Quadra 35**

HISTORICAL:

The Fairchild PT-19 (also designated as PT-23 and PT-26 and dubbed the 'Cornell') was a two-seat primary trainer used by both Canada and the U.S. during WWII. A low-winged monoplane, it was powered with a six-cylinder Ranger in-line, air-cooled engine of 175 hp. (The '23 had a 'round' Continental of 220 hp.) The Canadian version (PT-26) often had enclosed greenhouse cockpits, while U.S. '19's left the crew out in the slipstream. The enclosed variation was most probably a concession to extreme Canadian winters.

A very 'friendly' aircraft to fly, the '19 buzzed along at 113 mph, cruise, with a max of 125. Stable as a rock, it was easy to land with it's wide tread landing gear. Aerobatically, it was capable of most maneuvers of the rolling and looping kind, but it was not as adept as the Stearman PT series. Cadets who trained on PT-19's, followed by basic training in BT-13's (The 'Vultee Vibrator') had a rough time in single engined advanced training in AT-6's -- with ground loops!

Span was 36' 11 3/16", length was 27' 11 3/8". The airplane stalled at 54 mph, flaps out. The PT-19 was built in the U.S. by both Fairchild and Aeronca, until production was halted in late 1943. The 'round-engined' PT-23 was built by the Howard Aircraft Co., the Aeronca Co., and the St. Louis Aircraft Corp. (Formerly Curtiss) Canadian PT-26's, powered by 200 hp L-440-7 Rangers, were built by Fleet Aircraft Ltd., in Toronto, Ontario, until May of 1944.

PLAN:

Jim Folline's plan for the PT-19 was among the early plans designed after the advent of the Quadra 35 engine. The set consists of three very large plan sheets, 3 X 8 feet. The plan is extremely well done. It has several quite excellent isometric views and is complete with a printed instruction manual covering the fairly complicated wing construction right on the plan sheets. Certainly one of the first (and one of the best) plans around. An engine larger than the Q35 would improve the model's performance and the extra power will provide some safety factor as well.

The fuselage is typical stick construction although with a difference. 1/4 X 1/2 inch material is used on edge. That is, the 1/2 inch dimension is vertical to the building board. This makes quite a strong structure and the material bends easily to the contours required. The fuselage side frames then have a doubler added and this requires their being clamped into a curved shape while the glue between the fuselage side and the doubler sets up. This sounds complicated but is shown quite clearly on an isometric. The material used in the fuselage may be spruce or basswood, whichever is most convenient.

Landing gear wires require some digging to obtain the dimensions as they are shown on more than one sheet, but not completely on any sheet. The wire used is two thicknesses of 7/32 inch wire for each gear leg. Bending it will require considerable care in order to produce the required shapes which match one another.

The steerable tail-wheel is made from the plan and will take some metal working skill to fabricate. This work requires brazing and the making of several small parts. Excellent detail is shown on the plan for this mechanism.

Tail group members are conventional construction. They require a number of shaped parts to be made up before actual construction can begin. Control surface areas are large and will provide excellent control even at fairly low speeds.

The servos for rudder and elevator are mounted in the rear of the fuselage, near the bottom front edge of the vertical fin. Long servo leads will be needed to reach them so the receiver antenna should be located as far away as convenient from these servo leads.

The wing is made in three sections; a center section which bolts to the fuselage and two outer sections which plug into the center section. The center section contains the landing gear so the model will sit on it's own gear without the outer sections in place.

Actual wing construction is pretty well standard model practice. The method of attaching the wings is unusual and will require considerable skill to make up. A number of small parts and even a special tool are needed. Many parts will require metal working abilities. Good isometrics show the complicated areas in detail.

Both flaps and ailerons are shown, the flap servo(s) are not, and consideration should be given to the use of two servos, one for each flap. Aileron servos are shown mounted at the inboard end of the ailerons and will therefore require long servo leads for connection to the receiver. The connections are mounted at the rib locations of the joint between the wing sections and are set up to be made, automatically, as the outer sections are mated. The use of long servo leads may require Ace Noise Traps, or equivalent if the radio being used is subject to interference generated by the long leads.

DEGREE OF DIFFICULTY:

Definitely not for the beginner or low time plans builder. The Folline PT-19 will stretch the abilities of all but the dedicated scale builder. It will require a good deal of quite delicate and exacting work to complete. Our rating of '4' leans toward a '5'. Good looking model!

1/4 SCALE

FIESELER STORCH (Fi-156 C-1)

FROM: Flugtechnik, Postfach 43, 7315 Weilheim-Teck, West Germany

SPAN: 146" CHORD: 18 1/2" DOD: 5 AREA: 2700 Sq. In.

LENGTH: 99" WEIGHT: 33# ENGINE: Bully 45 (3 HP)

HISTORICAL:

The Fieseler Storch would be difficult to mistake for any other airplane. It's high stance, narrow and menacing looking cowling and the mechanical complexity of it's wing structure give it a distinctive appearance closely resembling it's namesake, the stork.

The first prototype was flown in the spring of 1936 and the airplane served with the Luftwaffe from 1938 until 1945. It served with almost every major unit in virtually every theater of operations from Africa to Russia. The Storch served with the air forces of a dozen different nations, including Switzerland, Sweden, Spain and the USSR.

The advanced technology in the Storch's wing, consisting of leading edge slats and slotted flaps, permitted take-off runs of 230 feet and landings using only 85 feet of runway or less. The German Aviatrix, Hanna Reitsch often flew a Storch and, in early 1945, just prior to the fall of Germany, she landed one on a cleared street in Berlin, delivering messages to Hitler.

The Storch, originally intended as an army co-operation, reconnaissance, ambulance and communications airplane, became the personal transport of many senior German military officers. It's ability to get into (and out of) quite restricted landing strips made it more than a little popular.

PLAN:

The four sheet plan, no building manual, is all in German and the sizes are called out in metric measure. These two facts alone will produce some difficulty in construction. It may be necessary to modify some of the parts to accommodate non-metric sizes. The plans sheets are small in comparison to what we are used to seeing in larger models and would approximate three plan sheets in the usual North American plan set.

The Storch is a large model and the engines which will both fit into the narrow cowling, and provide adequate power, are few. The Bully 45 recommended is not the same Bully we are familiar with, so it should not be assumed that the Bully engine available in North America will fit the model. Careful consideration should be given to the choice of engine in order to power the Storch adequately and still conceal the model engine as much as possible. The depth of the cowl at the engine location is only eight inches and it's maximum width is about the same. The problem is the somewhat pear-shaped cowl with the wider part to the bottom.

The rather small size of the plan sheets has caused the designer to split the fuselage into two parts. This is not the problem it might seem, as the construction of the fuselage is somewhat unusual. The formers are assembled on a section of PVC tubing which will require careful alignment of the formers as the longerons are added. It is not obvious that the PVC tubing can be removed after the fuselage is framed, but this would seem to be a good idea in order to reduce the weight if for no other reason.

This method of construction has some advantages, but requires that the tubing on which the formers are placed be absolutely straight. As the sizes shown are metric, it will be necessary to choose a tubing size and cut the holes in the formers to match the tubing, rather than using the sizes shown on the plan. The formers are a foam material, where only shape is required, and one of the foam core materials could be used here.

The cabin area slopes outward from the top, then back in about halfway to the floor. This construction is aided by the shape of the formers, but will require some painstaking work to get it looking right.

The tail group is conventionally assembled, although some unusual materials are used. The ribs are made from a foam material (Foam Core could be used) and the outer edges of the tail members are made from a plastic material although balsa could be used here. All ribs are shaped, so a considerable number of different parts must be patterned and made.

The landing gear is a very complicated set-up and a number of metal parts will have to be fabricated to duplicate the original. Some experience and ability in metal working will be required to make the parts necessary for the landing gear and for the manufacture of a number of other fittings needed.

Only one wing panel is shown, so it will be necessary to build the other wing on the reverse of the plan. The wing uses a PVC tube as a spar (and this should NOT be removed after assembly). The square stock which holds the ribs in place is 5mm square which is slightly smaller than 1/4 square, but the slots may be enlarged and 1/4 used with little difficulty. These should be spruce, rather than balsa.

There is a lot of structure in these wings, complicated by the leading edge slats and the way the flaps deploy. It will be necessary to make up some metal fittings here as well. No servo installation is shown, but it is recommended that a separate servo be used for each control, in each wing panel.

DEGREE OF DIFFICULTY:

This is a very difficult model requiring considerable skill and experience. Several novel construction methods are used. Definitely not for anyone but the dedicated scale builder with plenty of experience. Our '5' is fully justified!

1/4 SCALE

FLEET FINCH

FROM: Len Bosman, 193 Baltic St., Coquitlam, B.C., Canada. V3K 5G9

SPAN: 84"   CHORD: 12"   DOD: 3   AREA: 2016 Sq. In.

LENGTH: 65"   WEIGHT: 20# +/-   ENGINE: QUADRA 35

HISTORICAL:

The Fleet Finch was used as a Royal Canadian Air Force trainer between the years of 1938 and 1941. During this period, more than 600 were built in Canada. Many of these airplanes still exist and either have been restored to flying condition or are in the process of restoration. A particularly good looking example is owned by the Edmonton Flying Club of Edmonton, Alberta.

The Finch can trace its lineage back through the Fleet Model 1 and Model 2, built in the U.S. in the late 20's and early 30's. Fleet airplanes had a reputation for great strength and proved it many times. In the early days of aviation, an airplane which could do an outside loop was perceived as a very strong machine. Paul Mantz, of movie fame, performed 46 consecutive outside loops in a Fleet in 1930. Civilian versions of the Fleet biplane were sold for the munificent price of $5,750, in the late 30's.

PLAN:

This two sheet plan by Len Bosman was among the first of his efforts. While the plan does not present the tidy appearance of those produced by more experienced designers, it does provide all the information required to build the model.

In his earlier plans, Bosman used some material which was significantly larger than necessary. The Finch's fuselage shows this with the use of 1/2 by 1/4 inch framing material. This is almost double the size needed, providing proper material is used and adequate glue joints are provided.

The fuselage construction is conventional except for the sizes used, and should not be difficult for anyone with a little experience. Spruce is called out on the plan and should be used. The firewall is laminated from four thicknesses of 1/4 inch plywood, and this too is 'overkill' as a half-inch lamination would be quite adequate.

Bosman has come up with a somewhat flexible motor mounting method similar to that used by Hostetler. In this case, two different sizes of hose are used along with 1/4-20 by 2 inch bolts. This method of vibration isolation looks very good indeed and should work very well.

Tail group members are conventionally constructed over the plan although the stabilizer and elevator are built up on 1/8 inch balsa sheet. The construction method shown is one of the easiest the authors have seen for this type of structure and should not be a problem.

Landing gear and cabane wires are specified as 1/4 inch piano wire. It goes without saying that a robust wire bender will be required to fabricate parts from such wire. Neither are shown as full sized patterns so careful measurement and accurate bending will be required in order to produce the shapes and sizes needed.

The wing structure, as might be expected, is quite adequately built for the intended loads. Two 1/4 X 1/2 inch and two 1/4 X 1/4 inch spars are used plus some additional 1/4 square around the ailerons in the lower wing. Seventy-four (!) wing ribs are required, so a good deal of time will be spent cutting them.

Ailerons are present only on the lower wing, so the single servo shown will be adequate. (The Finch was not a startling performer in it's original form, so the model should be flown at something less than 'pattern' speeds.) A method of transferring movement from the servo to the aileron using a torque tube is shown and apparently works well. It is important to use a material here which does not deform or twist as torque is applied, as such deformation will reduce the aileron movement.

While not difficult building, there is a good deal of it in the wings and their accurate assembly will take time. Both wings are built in one piece. At exactly seven feet in length, they will not be too difficult to transport.

Wing mounting uses nylon bolts, at front and rear, on the lower wing and the upper bolts to the top of the cabane struts. The method shown for housing these upper wing bolts inside the wing is through the use of common nuts, glued into slots in balsa blocks. The authors would use plywood plates and blind nuts although the method shown has been successfully used on a number of models without failure.

There have been a considerable number of Finches built from these plans in the designer's local area. The model flies very well and looks very good in the air, which has added to it's popularity, of course. The original known to the authors is painted 'peril' yellow, with RCAF markings, so it is a highly visible model wherever it is shown or flown.

DEGREE OF DIFFICULTY:

Bosman's Finch should not create any difficulty for anyone with a kit or two behind them, so long as the ability is present to make patterns and cut accurate parts and then assemble them properly. An attractive model will be the result. Our rating of '3' leans slightly in the direction of a '2'!

1/5 SCALE

GRUMMAN F8F 'BEARCAT'

FROM: Nick Ziroli, 29 Edgar Drive, Smithtown, New York. 11787

SPAN: 86"   CHORD: 24 1/2" - 10 1/2"   AREA: 1480 Sq. In.

LENGTH: 69"   WEIGHT: 20 - 30#   DOD: 4   ENGINE: 2 - 4 Cu. In.

HISTORICAL:

The Bearcat was Grumman's last propeller-driven fighter. Grumman's Navy fighter airplanes had a reputation for being able to absorb severe punishment and survive. The Grumman plant at Bethpage, Long Island, was known as the 'Bethpage Iron Works' by numerous Navy pilots who owed their lives to this ability to take it on the chin and still get back to base.

The Bearcat was designed to be a replacement for the F6F Hellcat and was meant to achieve performance which would surpass any possible Japanese development late in WWII. First deliveries to the Navy began in early 1945, but the Bearcat was not fated to see action. Some additional production contracted with General Motors was therefore cancelled.

The Bearcat, in it's production form, was more than 2000 pounds lighter than the Hellcat. It's R-

2800-34W P & W radial engine of 2100 HP, gave it a top speed of 425 MPH, with a range of 2000 miles at cruise power. Armament was reduced as well to just four .50 caliber wing mounted machine guns. It was able to carry two 2000 pound bombs, four five inch rockets or two Tiny Tim rockets.

A total of 1266 F8F's were built, some of them after WWII had ended, and many were sold as surplus, finding their way into racing circles. Daryl Greenameyer's F8F set several records although it was far from a stock airplane as it was raced. Plenty of good documentation material is available on both the Navy version and several racing versions of the Bearcat, including the Al Williams' Gulfhawk III, the last of a long line of special aircraft bearing the same name.

PLAN:

Ziroli's plan for the F8F is on four sheets and includes a set of construction photos as an aid to assembly. The plan sheets are the usual Ziroli quality; clear and easy to read, all the detail the experienced modeler will require to build the model is present on the plan sheets. Not a model for the rank newcomer to plans building. Nor will it be an easy model to fly. The full-scale machine was a hot airplane and the model will be even more so.

One plan sheet consists entirely of patterns, of which there are many. Some of these are quite large, so a good deal of pattern making and parts cutting is required. Full sized formers are shown so it's not necessary to retrace half formers in order to produce the parts needed.

Most formers and many parts are poplar plywood, a material which Ziroli uses extensively in his designs. (This material is the same as Sig's Lite-Ply.) As with many of his other designs, the Bearcat is built over a crutch which provides a good support for the fuselage and assures it's assembly will be aligned properly.

While the Quadra 35 engine is shown on the plan. With the wide variance possible in finished weight, it would be well to use a larger engine.

A considerable number of 1/8 by 1/4 inch stringers are required over the formers to give the model it's shape. This is then sheeted (planked) with 1/8 inch balsa. It will take a generous quantity of 1/8 inch sheet to cover this relatively large model, so be prepared for a good deal of strip cutting in order to make up the planking required. An excellent method of surfacing, strengthening and finishing such a model is to use a very light fiberglass cloth and resin over the prepared surface. A cloth weighing 0.6 ounces per yard is available from Dan Parsons Products in Albuquerque, N.M.

Tail feathers are conventional construction and, although are airfoil shaped, should not be a serious problem to those who have some building experience.

The landing gear shown is fixed and some alterations will need to be 'horse-back engineered' before construction of the wing is started if retract gear is to be fitted. This too, is work for the experienced only. Remember, retraction of the gear will transfer the weight of the wheels and part of struts aft. This could upset the balance of the model, so balance should be checked with gear both extended and retracted. It may be necessary to compromise slightly in order to attain an optimum balance point. Avoid placing the CG too far aft as this will make for a "squirrely" airplane.

Flaps are shown and will certainly help make the airplane a lot 'tamer' in the landings if they are used. A 180 degree retract servo is recommended for the flaps as considerable movement is required, not to mention the power necessary to move the large flaps out into the slipstream. Details of the flap mechanism are clearly shown on the plan.

Only one aileron servo is shown and, if only one is to be used, it should be powerful. A better idea would be to use one servo for each aileron. The aileron mechanism is shown on the plan and uses long linkages and bellcranks.

As the wing is tapered, a considerable number of wing ribs will have to be patterned and cut. There are 14 ribs, so two of each must be made. The wing is shown as being constructed in one piece, but with its moderate span, the model should not be too much of a problem to transport.

DEGREE OF DIFFICULTY:

Our '4' indicates this is not a model for the low time builder or flyer. It will require a good deal of work to build and finish and will test the modeler's skill on the 'sticks' as well.

1/5 SCALE

AT-6 'TEXAN' (BRITISH HARVARD)

FROM: NICK ZIROLI PLANS, 29 Edgar Drive, Smithtown, New York, 11787

SPAN: 102" CHORD: ROOT 18 1/4" TIP 10 1/2" AREA: 1500 Sq. In.

LENGTH: 71" WEIGHT: 25-30 # DOD: 4 ENGINE: 2-4 C.I.

HISTORICAL:

The AT-6 Texan (British Harvard) was originally built as a relatively inexpensive trainer, used mainly for transition between primary trainers and operational fighter aircraft. The Texan had some of the handling characteristics of a fighter, had retractable landing gear, and saw wide usage with about fifteen thousand built.

First produced as the BC-1 in 1938, it was a development of the BT-9 Basic Trainer. Power was a 600 HP Pratt and Whitney R-1340 radial engine which gave a top speed of 208 MPH. Seating was for two pilots in tandem. Wingspan - 42 feet, length - 29 feet. The airplane was produced right into the 1950's and saw combat in Korea as an air-strike spotter.

The AT-6 has seen wide service, having been used by many NATO countries as both a trainer and an operational aircraft. Some examples are still in service with some of the world's smaller air forces.

Many Texans and Harvards have been bought up by military historical groups and by individuals with an interest in military aviation. Many of these in private and institutional hands have been lovingly restored to better than new condition. They are being flown on a regular basis for pleasure and in air shows around North America. For this reason, really good documentation is readily available on the airplane almost anywhere. In the hands of a private pilot, the AT-6 provides a great deal more performance than the usual run-of-the-mill civil aircraft. Such performance does not come cheaply as the engine burns 45 gallons of aviation gasoline an hour.

PLAN:

The plan for Ziroli's Texan is well done as is to be expected from such a meticulous designer. The plan consists of four sheets, with some building instructions on the various sheets. No instruction booklet is provided and some experience is required to build Ziroli's Texan. It should certainly not be tackled by an inexperienced beginner.

A considerable amount of pattern making and parts cutting will be necessary as there are many wing ribs and fuselage parts which will require careful transferring of outlines to a pattern and then to the building material. Building from the plan will require a considerable quantity of material. Much of the model is balsa sheeted and even making the parts will require a large stock of flatwood in various sizes and thicknesses. Balsa and plywood is used extensively.

The fuselage is built on a crutch which assures the finished structure will conform to the required shape and that it will have considerable strength.

The wing is built in three sections, the center section containing the landing gear may be left on the model during transport so the model will sit on it's own gear. The installation of Dave Platt retracts is shown on the plan, or the model may be fitted with the usual stiff wire legs. The retracts add a good deal to the appearance of the model in the air and a competition model should have the retractable gear on board.

Both left and right wing panels are shown on the plan sheets. Wing joining is through a 1 1/4 inch aluminium tube which is claimed to be readily available through hardware stores. This method has considerable strength although it requires care in gluing the wood wing parts to the aluminium tubing.

One entire plans sheet contains nothing but patterns for parts required and there are others on other sheets. Be prepared for a lengthy session of pattern making and parts cutting when you begin construction.

Ziroli has the Texan available as a kit as well as in plan form. The fuselage is a well made in fiberglass. The wing is in kit form with all the wood, patterns and material required to build up the wings. This is more costly than building from the plan, but once all the costs are figured in, using the glass fuselage will not be significantly more costly than buying all that wood and doing all that work!

Several accessories are available. There is a vacuum-formed canopy available and it is of excellent quality. To make one's own, as opposed to buying the readily-available canopy, shouldn't even be considered! The canopy available from Ziroli is worth the added cost. A cowl is also available for the Texan and, in comparison to making up a cowl from wood, the glass cowl is the way to go. Much less time spent on it and there is much more room inside it for whatever engine is used.

A 2.44 c.i. Kioritz engine is shown on the plans and this is about the smallest engine that should be installed. This model can come out rather heavy, so extra power will be useful. A careful watch should be maintained during construction to assure that excessive weight is not added. (Scale airplanes absorb weight right out of the air!)

Optional flap construction is shown on the plan and their addition would probably make the T-6 a better flying (and landing) model.

DEGREE OF DIFFICULTY:

While the construction is relatively straightforward, there is considerable cutting of parts to be done. It is recommended that some experience be gained before tackling such a large and complex project. The Texan will also be a fairly hot flying model. It is not for the low-time pilot.

1/4 SCALE

RYAN XPT-16

FROM: Len Bosman, 193 Baltic St., Coquitlam, B.C. Canada. V3K 5G9

SPAN: 90" CHORD: 14" DOD: 3 AREA: 1250 Sq. In.

LENGTH: 64" WEIGHT: 17 - 20# ENGINE: QUADRA 35

HISTORICAL:

As World War II approached, the U.S. Army Air Corps felt the need for a new kind of primary trainer. The old biplane PT's didn't represent the kind of aircraft - low wing all-metal monoplanes - that were entering the combat squadrons. Adapting existing civilian trainers to military requirements seemed to be the way to go. Ryan aircraft was manufacturing a beautiful little trainer with an all-metal fuselage and fabric covered flying surfaces that held a lot of promise -- the STA. In early 1939, the Air Corps contracted for a single Ryan XPT-16. It was delivered in June. The XPT-16 was a "militarized" STA powered by a 4-cylinder Menasco C-4 engine of 125 Hp. It spanned 30 feet; was 21 feet 5 1/2 inches long and 6 feet 8 1/2 inches high. It had to be "hand-propped" to start (a self-starter was added, later). Its tandem cockpits held dual controls as well as military instrumentation. The wings and tail surfaces were wire braced. Max speed was 150 mph and the '16 cruised at 127. Its service ceiling was 17,500 feet.

The Menasco engine proved to be a bit fragile for the beating it took in military training service so it was decided to replace it with a Kinner B-5 radial of equal power (thus requiring a redesignation of the aircraft to "XPT-16A"). The streamlined wheel pants and strut fairings were removed to facilitate maintenance. The "A" continued in service until it was salvaged in June of 1941; after 1023 hours of flying time. It "sired" over 1500 more Ryan primary trainers for the Air Corps.

PLAN:

This two sheet plan from Bosman is his usual standard. No building manual is supplied. For this reason, some building experience will be an asset.

The fuselage is conventional construction. Bosman has a tendency to 'over-build' a little and this is obvious in the size of the material used to make up the fuselage. The main longerons are 1/4 X 1/2 inch spruce and the remainder of the stick material is the same size, in balsa. This could be reduced to 1/4 square or 1/4 X 3/8 inches without any real sacrifice in strength. The addition of light plywood gussets at all fuselage joints will more than make up for the reduction in material sizes.

Due to the cylindrical shape of the fuselage, there are a good many formers to be cut. Planking will be required to preserve the appearance of the original, and this will be rather painstaking work to assure proper fit of the strip planking. Considerable pattern making and parts cutting is needed in the construction of this model.

The Quadra engine is shown mounted and a vibration isolation mount is made using hose material, similar to a method used by Wendell Hostetler on his plans.

The landing gear is a little complicated and makes use of a spring loaded shock absorbing strut. This will require some skill with metal working tools and some experience with the fabrication of small parts. This landing gear is quite ingenious in it's imitation of the original and also as a means of absorbing landing shocks. Since it 'shows' on the completed model, careful work here will be rewarded in "static points".

The fin and rudder are standard built up construction and the stabilizer and elevator are made on 1/8 inch balsa sheet with strip stock simulating ribs.

Wing construction is a little out of the ordinary in that light cardboard is used for the sheeting at the leading edge. The wing is fabricated in two panels and then joined, using dihedral braces to make a solid joint. Some trimming of the inboard edges of the main spars is required before or after joining takes place.

The light card stock is soaked in water for a short period before application. Substantial savings in material costs are possible through the use of such material, of course.

The use of torque tubes (flaps and ailerons) require careful selection of the material to be used. Any tendency of the material used to flex when rotated will cut down on the movement available at the operating end. The method used to transfer the movement to the ailerons will easily allow differential aileron movement to be provided by the placing of the drive stud in the end of the torque tube. This is not shown on the plan, but would be easily 'horse-back' engineered during construction.

A single heavy duty servo is shown for ailerons and two slightly lighter duty ones for the flaps, one each side.

The wing is constant chord so only a few patterns are needed and the ribs may be made using the stacking method. Dihedral is 4 1/2 inches, so this unique little monoplane should be quite stable in flight. Control surfaces are large enough to provide good maneuverability as well. Wing loading, at just over 37 oz/sq. ft. is getting up there but should still produce a fairly docile model. (Calculation is based on 20# finished weight)

DEGREE OF DIFFICULTY:

Our '3' indicates some experience is required here. Building the '16' should not be a problem to the experienced builder although there is a good deal of 'fiddly' detail work involved.

1/4 SCALE

STEARMAN PT-13/N2S-5

FROM: Barron's Scale Classics, 11506 Ohio Ave., Youngtown, Arizona. 85363

SPAN: 96 1/2" CHORD: 15" DOD: 5 AREA: 2500 Sq. In.

LENGTH: 75" WEIGHT: 24 # ENGINE: Quadra 35

HISTORICAL:

The Stearman primary trainer of WWII is sort of mis-named. Most of them were built by Boeing. who had bought out Lloyd Stearman's airplane factory. Also designated the PT-17, PT-18 and PT-27 (Stearman Model 75) the only essential differences were in the engines installed. Post-war modification included hanging a 450-horse 'round engine' on the front of the rugged military bipe. (In military trim, engines of around 220 HP were standard.) Putt-putting along at the usual leisurely 95 mph cruise of the Stearman, one wouldn't be aware of it's quite spectacular aerobatic capabilities. Even today, the bird is known as competitive wherever stunt pilots congregate. Slow rolls needed a slight dive, to 105 mph; loops require 120 'on the clock' before the big biplane will go over the top.

The only real problem with flying the PT, is the ever present danger of ground loops.

The close-set landing gear doesn't provide good directional control on the ground and scraped wing tips are not all that rare!

Both the Army Air Corps and the Naval training commands used the bird. The Navy designated it N2S-1 through 5. The Stearman was the first aircraft to be designated A/N -indicating some 'standardization' between the Army and Navy. Span is 32' 2" and length is 25' 1/4". When production of the Kaydet was concluded in February of 1945, some 10,346 of these rugged biplanes had been built.

PLAN:

Richard Barron was in the business of producing large plans a longer period of time than most. He had larger plans before almost anyone but Sid Morgan, and he has done some excellent work. This plan for the Stearman PT-13 is a monumental work, covering all five plan sheets and is accompanied by a 13 page, step-by-step builder's manual. This latter contains a comprehensive bill of materials. (Comprehensive is **the** word -- the builder can plan on the use of very significant quantities of balsa, spruce strip wood, plywood and brass tubing!) The PT-13 follows scale construction and dimensions very well. The designer claims the one deviation from accuracy from full scale is one degree less incidence of the upper wing. The fuselage is built up from hardwood dowel, to simulate the steel tubing structure of the original airplane.

Wing loading, at the specified finished weight of 24 pounds, would be just a tad over 22 ounces/square foot. Even if the model were to end up weighing 30 pounds (an increase over spec'd weight by 25 %) the wing loading would still be just under 28 ounces per square foot. This is still well within a loading which will provide good flying qualities.

With the exception of the material used (dowel stock), the fuselage structure is not very different from any other model. There is a lot more building to be done, of course, and it will be a bit tricky using dowels rather than the usual square stock. All the joints between the dowelling show 1/16 inch plywood gussets. Cutting these will provide hours of amusement to the dedicated scale builder. (Some of these gussets are of odd shapes, so considerable time will be needed to produce the 'special' ones.)

Those builders who delight in preparing patterns and cutting parts will also find considerable enjoyment in this model. The drawings show over 40 patterns required in the construction of the fuselage alone, not counting the interior fuselage formers!

Considerable metal-working is also required as there are a myriad of small metal parts to be made. These anchor flying and landing wires; make up the landing gear and provide for several of the other metal items needed to 'dress' the model fully.

The landing gear provides for a spring-loaded 'oleo' type shock absorbing function to smooth those hard landings on un-improved fields. Making this assembly will require some skill and the ability to work metal accurately. The tail wheel is also shown with a shock absorbing mounting. Some skill in metal working will also be required here, working on smaller parts.

Stabilizer span is almost 40 inches tip to tip -- greater than the wingspan of some smaller models. Some dowel stock is used in the stab, elevator, fin and rudder to approximate full scale structure. Care will be required to build accurate (and true) assemblies.

All five wing sections are shown on the plans. (five -- including the upper wing center section.) All wing spars are 'box' type spars, made up from quarter square spruce and 1/16 inch plywood. These will be very strong and will need to be made up carefully so that accurate sizes will be maintained. (The wing ribs will have to slide onto the spars during assembly.)

A total of almost 70 wing ribs will be needed to make the wings. Only ten patterns are needed from which the ribs will be made. Rib spacing is at scale dimensions and a significant number of small gussets is required for reinforcing the wing rib glue joint at the spars. (This model is well engineered and will be more than strong enough to survive some hard usage.)

DEGREE OF DIFFICULTY:

This is most definitely NOT a model for the faint-hearted or the low time builder. The true scale 'addict' will get a great deal of pleasure from building and flying this well-designed (and accurate to scale) model. Our mark of '5' indicates the amount of work required.

1/5 SCALE

VOUGHT CORSAIR, F4U-1

FROM: Nick Ziroli, 29 Edgar Drive, Smithtown, New York. 11787

SPAN: 93" CHORD: 19 1/2" Root - 13" Tip AREA: 1650 Sq. In.

LENGTH: 73 1/4" WEIGHT: 18 - 25# DOD: 4 ENGINE: Q35 - Q50

HISTORICAL:

The Corsair or F4U built by Chance-Vought, entered the Second World War in 1943. This was the last major production piston engined fighter and took advantage of all the engineering data and experience gained over the previous several years. In all, over 12,000 were built, including those manufactured by Brewster and Goodyear. They destroyed in excess of 2,000 enemy aircraft. Losses in compiling this record were a mere 189 aircraft.

Later versions of the Corsair (the F4U-4) were capable of almost 450 MPH from the 2450 HP double-row R-2800 Wasp engine. Range exceeded 1500 miles and it could carry two 1000 pound bombs in addition to eight rockets and six .50 caliber machine guns. Some models were fitted with four 20 mm cannon. Wingspan was 42 feet, length 33 feet. 8 in., making for a very large single seat fighter airplane. It is claimed the Corsair was superior to the Mustang above 12,000 feet.

The distinctive inverted gull-wing of the Corsair, designed to permit ground clearance for the large diameter propeller, assures little chance of mistaken identity. There is no other airplane which looks just like a Corsair!

Some of these 'bent winged birds' found their way into civilian hands following their retirement from military service. They have been lovingly restored to 'as new' condition and are maintained by groups and individuals in flying condition. Excellent documentation is readily available for the F4U.

PLAN:

The four sheets of the Ziroli plan are crammed with information and a set of photo data sheets is included. One plan sheet includes all of the patterns required so the construction plan need not be destroyed for patterns. A cowling, canopy and a 'Corsair Style' Quadra spinner are available from Ziroli.

Ziroli's experience shows in the plan sheets. He has done an excellent job on the F4U. There is a good deal of information on the building of the Corsair on the plan sheets and no building instruction set, as such, is offered.

The fuselage is built on a crutch which is specified as 'hardwood'. It is safe to assume that what is actually meant is a softwood such as spruce and it would certainly be adequate to build the crutch from such material. This crutch is then supported up off the building board and the formers are assembled to it. This is a little out of the ordinary as far as construction methods are concerned, and care must be taken to assure that all formers are vertical to the crutch. A belt-drive .60 is shown on the plan, along with a Q35 installation. A better selection of engine would be one of the larger gas-burners. The authors have seen a Q50 powered version of the model fly and it was off the ground after a remarkably short run, estimated at 50-75 feet.

The landing gear shown is fixed wire gear bent from 7/32" wire, with 1/8" wire braces. There are now some commercially available 90-degree retracts that fit this model and they add considerably to it's good looks. Keep in mind that the gear folds rearward and thus transfers weight aft as it folds. This transfer of weight will have to be taken into account when the model is being balanced to put the CG in it's proper place. The transfer of weight to the rear could have a dramatic effect on the performance of the model in flight.

The fuselage may be covered with one of the usual covering materials or may be sheeted. This latter is the preferred method. The original airplane was aluminium skinned and cloth just doesn't measure up. A light cloth and resin finish may be added over the sheet stock and this will provide a very tough (and smooth) surface for finishing. (NOTE: the O.6 oz. glass cloth sold by Dan Parsons Products is ideal for this.)

The wing folding mechanism is shown on the plan and makes a good looking addition to the model. Folding the wings is not power-operated as in the full scale version. It's strictly requires the 'Armstrong' method.

One of the difficulties of building the Corsair is the wing center section which provides the distinctive shape of the wing. The outer wing panels are straight; it is the center section which is of an unusual shape and which must be built, not only accurately, but strongly as well. Directions are included on the plan to build the wing in one piece. Why anyone would want to do this is hard to say.

The major difficulty in the Corsair is the making of the veritable dozens of patterns, transferring them to the material and then cutting accurate parts. The pattern sheet is literally crammed with parts to be made and many of them are quite large. Be prepared for a good deal of painstaking work and the use of a good deal of material.

Considering the popularity of WWII fighter airplanes, the Corsair fits right into that era and is a little out of the ordinary when compared to the many Mustangs which abound at most club fields. This is a large and impressive bird which performs very well on a Q5O or equivalent engine.

DEGREE OF DIFFICULTY:

Due to the complex wing shape, the method of fuselage construction and the many, many parts required, a rating of four out of five is in order. This will not be a model to be risked in the air by the Sunday flier. Some skill 'on the sticks' will be needed to fly it well and realistically.

1/5 SCALE

KINGFISHER (OS2-U)

FROM: Douglas McBrien, 24 Truby St., Granby, Mass. 01033

SPAN: 86" CHORD: 21 5/8" - 13 1/4" AREA: 1140 Sq. In.

LENGTH: 69 1/2" WEIGHT: Unspecified DOD: 5 ENGINE Q35 - 50

HISTORICAL:

Vought Aircraft Company's new design for 1937 ultimately was named the 'Kingfisher'. It was to replace aging biplane scout airplanes in the inventory of the Navy. It featured the ability to be switched from a wheeled landplane to a single-float seaplane. Its first duties were as a catapult-launched scout, from the decks of battleships and light cruisers. Three were normally carried on the former; two on the latter. The normal OS2U compliment of aircraft carriers was four.

Power for the Kingfisher was the Pratt & Whitney R-985-48, and the first fifty-four OS2U-1's were delivered in 1940. It spanned 35 ft. 10", was 30 ft. 1" long and 12 ft. 11" high. Subsequent 'dash 2' and 'dash 3' versions were produced during World War II, the essential differences being in added armor protection for the crew, more powerful engines (P&W 985-50 and 985

AN-2). Vought produced 1,006 of the 'dash 3' version; the Naval Air Facility, 300.

As WW II progressed many new missions were found for the Kingfisher. Most prominent was its use as an Air Search and Rescue plane for the Navy. In this role, its most famous "save" was that of Capt. Eddie Rickenbacker, WW I ace. 'The Bug', piloted by Lt. Bill Eadie, was instrumental in locating Capt. Eddie and two companions, who had been in a rubber raft for 22 days. With one survivor in the back seat and both others lashed to the wings, Lt. Eadie was unable to take off. He proceeded to taxi 60 miles over rough seas to safety.

PLAN:

McBrien's monumental four sheet plan is an impressive sight when they are first unrolled. There seems to be **acres** of paper covered with the details necessary to construct this striking and unusual airplane. The plan set includes an instruction manual and a set of very well done pictures which certainly help during the construction phase.

The Kingfisher is a huge model and looks even bigger on it's single large float (the wheeled version is also shown on the plan). This is no project for any but the dedicated builder who doesn't mind having to really 'read' a plan and who isn't daunted by great deal of work. All others should avoid this one! One or two balsa logs in the stock room wouldn't be a bad idea, either! Despite these minor reservations, the Kingfisher is a most impressive model, on the ground, in the water and in the air. It's not the type of model you'll encounter at every field within a hundred miles of home.

Basic construction is not for the newcomer to modeling, let alone the beginning plans-builder. This is a large and complex project and a good deal of reference to the plans and to the manual will be required.

Many formers are required, so considerable pattern making and parts cutting are necessary even before any real construction is begun. The method of building the fuselage is not the usual run-of-the-mill project. Its assembly is not clear from the plan sheets so the manual will be referred to almost continually.

The landing gear is shown on the plans and requires the making up of a shock absorber. The remainder of the wire parts are not complicated, although some tight bends are required in the trailing strut.

Tail group members are somewhat unusual in construction and will require skill and experience to build properly. The plan and instructions are quite clear as to the methods of assembly, but care should be taken to understand these methods clearly before **any** wood is cut.

The main float is larger than many model airplane fuselages and will require as much or more construction time as a similar sized model. Some metal work will be necessary in the making of the water rudder and the control system for it. The water rudder is important for any sort of reasonable control on the water and must be properly engineered to stand the use it will receive. The float pylons, which attach the model to the main float, will also require some parts cutting and care in assembly.

Small wing floats are also required in order to balance the model on it's main float while waterborne.

The wing is tapered, so it too will necessitate considerable pattern making and parts cutting. This section of the model is also a complex structure which will require considerable attention to both plan and building instructions for successful construction.

No flaps are shown and only one servo is shown for the ailerons. Keep in mind that the Kingfisher is NOT an aerobatic airplane and will not require separate aileron servos so long as one of adequate power is used.

It should be kept in mind during all construction on the Kingfisher that, if it is to be flown from water, it should be well protected from the inevitable spray which will result. All possible entry points for water should be properly sealed and ONLY glues which are **WATERPROOF** should be used.

DEGREE OF DIFFICULTY:

This is NOT a model for any but the dedicated scale builder. There is a considerable amount of work involved and the Kingfisher is not a model which will be completed in a few weeks. Our DOD of '5' tells it the way it is.

1/5 SCALE

WESTLAND LYSANDER

From: Len Bosman, 193 Baltic St., Coquitlam, B.C. Canada. V3K 5G9

SPAN: 127 3/4" CHORD: 14 3/8" (ROOT) 17 1/4" MAX AREA:1128 Sq.In.

LENGTH: 73" WEIGHT: UNKNOWN DOD: 4 ENGINE: QUADRA 35

HISTORICAL:

The Westland Lysander was first flown June 15, 1936 and was designed as a liaison aircraft for the British Royal Air Force. The airplane is very large for a single engined aircraft and sits very high, giving a quite imposing impression with it's bulk. Quite distinctive in appearance with an unusual wing planform, bulky looking landing gear housings and large fuselage, it is an aircraft impossible to mistake for any other.

The full scale airplane was equipped with a Bristol Mercury XX radial engine of 870 BHP, quite powerful for it's time. The engine was a complex piece of engineering with almost 2200 moving parts. Weight of the airplane was 5800 pounds and, with full tanks, it had a range of 400 miles. A large auxiliary tank could be fitted, dramatically extending the range.

The Lysander was equipped with a novel, and for the time, quite advanced set of slots, slats and flaps which gave it STOL characteristics long before the word was coined. The outer slats popped out independent of any control by the pilot, at around 60 MPH. Then, at a slightly slower speed, the inboard slats and the flaps were deployed at the same time, automatically. This could lead the unwary or inexperienced pilot into the "rocking horse game" where the airplane alternately climbed and dived in concert with the operation of all that laundry popping in and out. Speed changes caused the mechnical paraphenalia to go through it's routine. The Lysander was used extensively in clandestine operations into Occupied Europe, working with the underground.

PLAN:

The Bosman Lysander plan consists of four plan sheets, with construction notes and instructions right on the drawings. No building booklet is included, but the experienced builder will have no problem with the model. It is not a plan for the newcomer to plans construction and should be left until the builder has gained a good deal of experience in construction. The unusual shape of the wing, the method of mounting the wings (which are two separate sections) may be more than the newcomer should tackle as a first-time project.

The method of operating the flaps, using glass tubing or similar materials, may result in a significant amount of "play" in this mechanism. Be sure to use a material here which will not deform badly when torque is applied. A reduction of flap movement could result. Len Bosman, the designer, had one flap become inoperative due to a mechanical failure and this made the model very difficult to control. While all control system components should be made as precise as the builder can, the flap operating mechanism should receive careful planning and workmanship to avoid any problems. The automatic slats, coupled with, and which operate the flaps, would be a very real challenge to the model builder. Len's plan does not show the slats, although the flaps are shown and can be made operable.

Fuselage construction is principally hard balsa. The sizes called out on the plan are quite large. It would be possible to use a good quality spruce (Sitka, for example) and reduce the sizes used significantly. The use of spruce would increase the strength of the fuselage in all likelihood and reduce the model's building cost.

The balance of the Lysander's construction is quite straight-forward although not for the beginner as noted above. Each wing panel is made in one piece and the flaps and ailerons cut out afterward, thus assuring a good fit. This method requires some experience in facing the cut edges. So if you have not done this sort of work before, be prepared to do some improvising. There are an amazing number of different sizes of wing and stabilizer ribs, so be prepared for a very great deal of pattern making and cutting of parts.

The Lysander, even at 1/5th full size, is a large and very impressive model. It will require a good deal of work, and lots of material Not for the faint-hearted -- but a beauty when completed. There are restored Lysanders at Wright-Patterson Air Force Museum, Dayton, Ohio, and at the RCAF Museum, Ottawa, Canada. Either of these aircraft are displayed so as to permit photos to be made for documentation purposes.

DEGREE OF DIFFICULTY:

In our rating system, the Lysander would be a four. Not for the low time builder! The main structures are not difficult to build. But considering the number of wing ribs required, the wire bending required for the wing mounting cradle and the making of the wheel pants and fairings, the model does require some skill.

1/3rd SCALE

DRUINE TURBULENT

FROM: Douglas McBrien, 24 Truby St., Granby, Mass. 01033

SPAN: 86 1/4"　CHORD: 15 7/8"　DOD: 3　AREA: 1369 Sq. In.

LENGTH: 59"　WEIGHT: UNDER 20#　ENGINE: Quadra 35

HISTORICAL:

Of French "extraction", the Turbulent is a light, single-place, low winged, fixed gear craft, designed to be home-built. It was designed by Roger Druine in the mid-50's and has been duplicated many times, both in Europe and the United States. It was/is intended for a relatively low-powered engine (of the converted Volkswagen aircooled 'Bug powerplant class).

Span of the craft is 21' 6" and it's 17 ' long. Wing area approximates 80 sq. ft. Engines of 30 to 40 horsepower engines are specified although power plants of up to 80 HP have been used. As is true of many home-built designs, the basic Turbulent has been modified to include such niceties as full-coverage cockpit canopies and wheel pants.

Since there are so many variations on the Turbulent theme, it is recommended that anyone modelling this aircraft either find a specific airframe to "copy" or contact Doug McBrien or one of the documentation services (noted in the **SOURCE** section of this book) for photographs of a Druine that appeals to them.

PLAN:

For a first plan, this Druine Turbulent by McBrien is extremely well done. McBrien has obviously been at the drafting table for some time and knows his way around it very well. The three sheet plan is complemented by both building notes and a series of construction pictures which are also well done. Although they aren't as slick as might come out of a kit box, they are well printed and are a real help during construction.

A good three-view of N417M is shown on the plan, along with its paint scheme. Although the actual colors used on the original are not detailed, they consist of black, white, and gold which don't present any difficulty in duplicating.

The full scale Turbulent is a relatively simple airplane and its smaller cousin is, naturally, similar. The fuselage shapes are not at all complicated, the only curved areas being the cowl top and the turtledeck.

The fuselage framework is 1/4 inch square spruce and balsa, gusseted where necessary. Sides of the fuselage are sheeted with a two-ply made up from 1/16 inch balsa and 1/32 inch plywood, with the plywood to the outside. This is a particularly strong arrangement and the model will withstand considerable hard use without fear of failure.

Formers required for fuselage construction are shapes which will not add any significant difficulty to building. With the exception of the forward cowl area and the turtledeck, all parts consist of straight lines.

The cowling is open at the bottom which provides superb cooling for the engine along with ease of manufacture of the cowling.

The tail group will require some extra effort during construction as all surfaces are airfoil shaped. The builder with some experience will have little difficulty. Control surfaces are huge (as in the original) and will provide excellent control at lower air speeds. No external bracing is required.

Wing construction is a little out-of-the-ordinary as the Turbulent uses leading edge slats. Construction details are well illustrated, and, aside from working with relatively small parts, this should not prove difficult.

A single large servo is shown for ailerons and is located in the wing center section. Two pushrods are used to connect the servo output arm to bellcranks at the aileron locations. This moves the ailerons through a solid, adjustable link. Care must be taken when installing the connecting pushrods between the servo arm and the bellcrank. These MUST be parallel to one another in their 'home' position. The reason for this is that, if they are not, one will become excessively tight and the other quite slack as the servo is moved away from center. This condition will place excessive stresses on the parts involved and could lead to eventual failure.

The plywood dihedral braces for the one-piece wing must be patterned and cut accurately, of course, in order to provide a wing which is symmetrical. This wing is quite strong and requires no external bracing or struts.

Elevator and rudder control-runs are interesting in that they use 45# test Steelon cable, running inside Gold-N-Rod outer sleeves. This provides a low co-efficient of expansion and the outer sleeves assure both ease of operation and proper positioning.

The landing gear wires are quite straightforward and should bend without difficulty. A scale landing gear strut cover is shown for those who wish to 'dress-up' the model.

DEGREE OF DIFFICULTY:

The Turbulent should present no problems for anyone with a kit or several behind them. Thus our '3'. The original model has been flown from wheels, floats and ski's. Flies very well (we've seen Doug's in the air) and it looks great. Good scale subject due to it's simplicity for detailing and it's flying qualities.

1/4 SCALE

ERCOUPE

FROM: Jim Messer's Model Products., 106 Valleyview Dr., Allegany, N.Y. 14706

SPAN: 90" CHORD:16" DOD: 3 AREA: 1250 Sq. In.

LENGTH: 61" WEIGHT: 17# ENGINE: Quadra 35

HISTORICAL:

Unique among U.S. light airplanes, the Ercoupe had no rudder pedals! It was a two-control airplane (elevators and coupled ailerons and rudder) and was "driven" by the pilot with a control wheel. The nose wheel of the tricycle landing gear was also steered by the same wheel for ground operations. It was claimed to be unspinnable -- and easy enough for the average automobile driver to fly!

The Ercoupe appeared in production numbers in 1940 after three years of flight testing. World War II interrupted manufacture but Erco's production line resumed construction in 1945. A low-wing all-metal monoplane, power for the Ercoupe included Continental engines of 65 to 85 horsepower. Wing span was 30 feet (airfoil: NACA 43013, 60 inch wing chord); length was 20 feet, nine inches; overall height was 5 feet, 10 inches. Max speed was a sizzling 110; cruise was 95 and landing speed was 37 mph. The design was certified on Edo floats as well as its tri-gear.

Ercoupes "soldiered" during WW II, as man-carrying aerial targets. Some Post-War versions had 90 Hp engines and were "dolled up" with wheel pants and sporty paint jobs. In 1948 began a strange and wonderful life for the Ercoupe design. Erco sold their interest to Bob Sanders, an Erco Sales Manager. Sanders/Ercoupes were built and sold until 1951, the Korean War interrupting production again. Sanders sold the design to Vest Aircraft in Colorado who built a few and then sold the design to Forney who sold out to Alon! Scale modelers are cautioned to document their replicas very carefully.

PLAN:

While Jim Messer may not have designed a large number of plans, the three sheets of his plan for the Ercoupe show a familiarity with the work and an economical use of the space. Nice plan, well drawn, and enough detail to allow construction of a fine model. Also included is a page of cautions which indicate areas where special care is required. The entire plan is letter-keyed to the parts patterns which assures ease of finding the parts when needed, but it will be necessary to mark the parts as they are made. (A good idea in any building project!) A three-view of NC 11691 is shown on the plan sheets without dimensions or color information. One plan sheet consists of the stab and elevator and all of the patterns required. These are well marked and there are a bunch of them!

The fuselage is built over a jig which consists of a single piece of 1 inch by 1/4 inch pine which is marked off the plan as to former locations. The jig is used for the basic fuselage lay-up and is then discarded. This 'jig' is rather light, so care must be taken to assure that it is supported up off the work surface in a flat plane. Any curvature in the jig will produce a similar curvature of the airplane. It is best to support it at several locations, checking from time to time to make sure it is dead flat before any gluing is done.

There is some ambiguity in the placing of the fuselage braces as the formers are mounted on the jig. (These are 'tack' glued to hold them in place until assembly is completed and the jig is then cut away and discarded.) While a little hard to read, the bracing can be sorted out with few minutes study. The real fun in building the fuselage comes when the stringers are added to the rear formers after basic assembly. There are 48 of them spaced around the fuselage and getting them in place will take a while. (78 feet of them, in total!). These are 1/8 square and, as spruce is recommended, a particularly strong fuselage will result.

Only the main landing gear patterns are shown, which is a pity. The nose gear is not shown but is available from Messer, made up and ready to mount. (A complete kit for the model is available as well.) There may be a nose-wheel gear which will fit in the Ercoupe and some shopping around may be in order to try to find one.

No cowling is available, but, as the upper fuselage extends right to the rear of the prop, only a small lower section of cowling is required. The plan recommends this be built from scrap balsa with the engine in place. (Be sure to close off the carb and exhaust port while doing this work. While a small quantity of balsa dust probably won't hurt your engine, why take a chance on something else getting into it?)

The tail members are fairly simple, although with two fins and two rudders, the linkage to drive the rudders is a little more complex than the usual methods used. The stab and elevator will require some care in assembly as the parts are made from material of a variety of thicknesses. (Shims are used under the parts to position them properly during assembly.) Control areas are generous and it is claimed the model is capable of extensive aerobatics.

The wing panels are built separately and then joined later. While no specified dihedral is shown, the dihedral braces will assure the correct amount. No mention is made of canting the inboard wing ribs to assure a good joint when the two halves are assembled. Working out the correct angle and then setting those ribs up accordingly will not be difficult and should certainly be done. The wing structure is well braced and should withstand any flight loads the model is capable of attaining.

DEGREE OF DIFFICULTY:

While the plan for the Ercoupe will be reasonably clear to anyone with some building experience, it is not for the beginner, thus our rating of '3'.

1/5 SCALE

GRUMMAN AG-CAT

FROM: Model Builder Magazine, 621 W. 19th St. Costa Mesa, California, 92627

SPAN: 89"(U) 82 1/2" (L) CHORD: 11 7/8" AREA: 2036 SQ.IN.

LENGTH: 51 3/4 WEIGHT: 18 POUNDS DOD: 3 ENGINE: 2 C.I. OR BELT DRIVE

HISTORICAL:

The Grumman Ag-Cat was designed in the late 1950's and was intended to take the place of the aging (and getting scarce) Stearman biplanes (PT-13's and PT-17's) which had been the mainstay of the agricultural spray business since the end of World War II.

Those Stearmans had done yeoman work, but the hard flying, and the corrosive atmosphere of the spray business had taken its toll. The aging Stearmans found new homes in the hands of restorers who have sent them back into the air in better-than-new condition.

The definitive design parameters for the Grumman Ag-Cat were to be: stability, ease of flying, simplicity of maintenance, and the safety of the pilot. This latter point has been amply confirmed out by the number of pilots who have 'bent' the Cat and walked away with minor injuries. The reputation of the "Grumman Iron Works" has changed little since the days when Hellcats and Wildcats poured out of the Bethpage works and headed for the Pacific, where they were to turn the tide of war against the Japanese. Grumman builds sturdy birds!

PLAN:

This Model Builder plan, designed by Floyd Fitzgerald, builds a chunky looking model, which is as it should be. The original Ag-Cat was a chunky, tough looking airplane. The plan consists of three sheets, plus a two page reprint of the magazine article with which it first appeared. The article is a lot of help in the building of the model and should be referred to as construction progresses.

Only the center section and right wing halves are shown on the plan which means the left wing panels will need to be built on the back of the plan. Not the most fun in the world but nothing to make a large fuss over.

There is not a great deal on the plan which will give any problems to anyone who has done some plans building. There is a good deal of construction required, but most of it is the usual run-of-the-mill model construction.

Large numbers of patterns will be required for all the parts needed and a great deal of preparation will need to be done before construction starts. If you make parts up as you go along, the time spent will not be as noticeable as if you make all the parts before beginning construction.

Using gussets on all the fuselage joints would add a great deal of additional strength to the fuselage without adding to the weight by any appreciable amount. We recommend it. The judicious use of spruce for the main fuselage structure would also add greatly to the strength with a minimal weight increase.

The designer has experimented with a spray device but no instructions are included on the plans for a scale spray rig. Such an arrangement would certainly add great realism to the flight of the Ag-Cat model.

He also recommends that a decision as to the degree of scale realism desired be made prior to the start of construction. To which we can add "AMEN". If a precision scale model is to be attempted, the gathering of documentation should be done before any wood is cut. In this way, the structure may be adapted during the early stages of construction in order to provide an accurate model. The plan is quite adequate for a Stand-Off or Sport Scale model.

While Floyd claims in the article which originally accompanied the plan in 1978 that he is not a builder or designer of any note, his work is certainly a cut-above the average. There is little, if anything, with which to find fault in the plan and it gives every evidence of being a design with some thought behind it.

DEGREE OF DIFFICULTY:

The Ag-Cat falls at about a three on our scale of five. It should be avoided as a first-time project, and probably it shouldn't be considered until a model builder has built and flown four or five such projects.

COMMENTS:

While the Ag-Cat looks as if it would be hard to manage in the air, because it looks so "short-coupled", the designer claims it flies in a stable and docile manner. While not specified as to displacement, the model was flown first on an O & R engine. This engine produced a measured 7 1/2 to 8 pounds of static thrust. This would be rather marginal for an 18 pound airplane and a Quadra 35 would produce about 12 pounds thrust with the same 18 X 6 propeller. The Quadra 35 engine, turning a 20 X 6 or 20 X 8 prop would be a much more capable source of power for the Ag-Cat at the weight specified.

PIPER PA-8 SKYCYCLE

FROM: Sid Morgan Plans, 13157 Ormond, Belleville, Michigan. 48111

SPAN: 60" CHORD: 15 1/2" - 10" DOD: 4 AREA: 600 Sq. In.

LENGTH: 45" WEIGHT: Unspecified ENGINE: .45 - .60

HISTORICAL:

The Piper Skycycle was the product of a miscalculation on the part of the Post-War planners. It was assumed that every returning military pilot would want his own small, single-place "flyabout". Unfortunately, they didn't and so the PA-8 was "an orphan".

Which is not to say that the Skycycle wasn't a fascinating airplane. It was constructed from an F4U drop tank! A large hole was cut atop the tank for the cockpit; an engine was hung on the front end and an aluminum boom was tacked on its back end. Voila, a fuselage! The engine was a Lycoming flat-four of 55 HP. The tiny bird got 32 miles per gallon (!) and had a range of over 400 miles from its 14-gallon fuel tank.

Wartime materials shortages were still limiting "civilian" aircraft construction so it wasn't unusual that **wooden** wings and tail feathers were designed and built. Span was a mere 20 feet! A wide-track landing gear was used to eliminate ground loops.

The tiny bird needed an outsized Plexiglas canopy because there wasn't much room left in the "drop-tank fuselage" to house the pilot. Despite the canopy's built-in headwind, the PA-8 perked right along, with a 120 mph top and a 95 mph cruise. Amazingly, the tiny craft was stressed to 7 G's!

PLAN:

This three sheet Sweitzer plan was designed in 1971, before the advent of the larger engines now in wide use. The Skycycle was meant to cater to those who wanted big, impressive models and, for it's day, the Skycycle was large.

At 60" span, the PA-8 is a small 1/4 scale model, today. It is also one which will present some difficulty to all but the experienced. The fuselage is built up on a series of three 'keels' and all formers but the firewall are cut in half, vertically, in order to be assembled to the main keel and the two side keels. This is work which will require some care to preserve the positions of the various parts and their relation to one another.

Once framed up completely, the fuselage is planked with 1/8 inch sheet stock. As the fuselage is round in shape, this will necessitate cutting a considerable amount of strip planking stock and then applying it to the fuselage. This is time consuming and tedious work. Be sure you are up to it before taking on the Skycycle. (If you like planking, you'll love this little airplane!). Light glass cloth and resin applied over the planking (after finish sanding) will provide both a smooth and tough surface for finish painting.

The tail assembly is all made of 3/16 inch balsa sheet, so is a simple matter of transferring patterns to the material and cutting out the shapes. Considerable sanding will be necessary in order to complete these for finishing, of course. Scale rib locations are shown if such detail intrigues the builder.

The landing gear is 3/16 inch wire and three bends are needed to make up the slightly complicated shape. Care will be needed to assure both are identical in shape. The gear mounts in the wings and the shape of the wire assures torque rod action to take up some of the shock of flying from rough ground. The gear leg fairing is shown and its addition to the model will provide a better appearance than the bare wires.

Wing construction is a little out of the ordinary as four ribs are laid in the wing diagonally (scale!) and only a few ribs run straight through the wing from leading to trailing edge. Quite a few parts are required, so a good deal of pattern making and parts cutting will be required before wing construction can begin.

Ailerons are of moderate size and are operated from one servo. This smaller model can safely be operated in this way, where it would not do for a larger one. Care should be exercised to assure that the aileron linkage has no excessive play in the control runs. Wing spars are 1/8 inch hard sheet balsa and are the full span of the wing, requiring the accurate cutting of 24 slots into which the ribs fit. Care will be required here to assure construction of a wing which is accurate to shape and in which each panel duplicates the other in reverse.

The wing is an interesting structure and will provide both some experience in unusual construction methods as well as a strong and reliable wing.

The Skycycle is a little out of the ordinary for a 1/4 scale model in that all the construction material is quite conventional, even if the methods are not. While quite small by today's standards, the Skycycle is a true 1/4 scale model and qualifies for such events. It is an unusual subject and one not to be seen at every scale rally or contest in the country. Simple instrumentation, a simple, colorful paint scheme and little external detail might suggest this model as a good beginner's scale subject. It is not!

DEGREE OF DIFFICULTY:

Our rating of '4' indicates that this is not a model for everyone. The assembly of the fuselage could prove to be frustrating for the inexperienced and may even give the experienced builder some exciting moments!

PIPER VAGABOND PA-15

FROM: Wendell Hostetler, 1041 Heatherwood Lane, Orrville, Ohio. 44667

SPAN: 114" CHORD: 19 1/4" DOD: 3 AREA: 2250 Sq. In.

LENGTH: 73" WEIGHT: 20 - 24# ENGINE: 2 - 4 H.P.

HISTORICAL:

A "meat-and-potatoes" airplane describes the Piper Vagabond to a "T". It was designed by Dave Long (who also engineered the Midget Mustang racer) in six weeks! Two seats, a 65 Hp Lycoming engine, fabric covering, a high wing and conventional landing gear, the Vagabond was aimed at WW II pilot and fixed base operator who wanted something that was inexpensive to buy, fly and maintain. It was priced at $1,990 fly-away, at Piper's Lock Haven, Penna. plant in mid-1948 with a plain yellow paint job. Wing span was 29 feet three inches (giving rise to the description of the Vagabond as the first of the short-winged Pipers). Chord was 63 inches; airfoil was the USA 35 M, as on other Pipers of the period. Over all length was 18 feet 8 inches and the Vagabond was an even 6 feet tall. It cruised at 92 mph (max speed 102) and landed at 45 mph. The Lycoming burned 4 gallons per hour from a

12-gallon tank. There were no shock absorbers in the landing gear system; fat airwheels took up the landing bumps. The full-swivelling spring-mounted tail wheel was steerable.

The Vagabond "sired" a host of other Piper designs. Among them were the Vagabond Trainer, the Clipper, the Pacer, the Colt and the tricycle-geared Tri-Pacer. Only a few accessory items were available for the Vagabond. Dual controls, a prop spinner and floor mats pretty well exhaust the optional items. Approximately 500 Vagabonds were made.

PLAN:

Hostetler's plans are usually well drawn and, more importantly, well engineered. The Piper Vagabond at 1/4 scale is no exception. His plans can be depended upon to produce good flying and long-lived models.

Two large sheets and a manual make up this plan for yet another of Mr. Piper's creations. The Vagabond is similar to most of the 'Cub' type airplanes built by Piper, but is a little more slender in the after part of the fuselage and has a rather large and quite distinctive fin and rudder.

The fuselage is built with 3/16 inch sheet balsa sides, reinforced inside with 1/4 X 3/8 inch strip wood (basswood specified, but spruce or other woods could be used). The 3/16 sheet stock parts required are quite large and it will be necessary to join several sheets in order to obtain the required 14 inch width.

The Kavan Twin engine and the 2.4 c.i. Kioritz are shown mounted, or one of the larger four stroke engines could be used with good results. The use of one of the physically larger gas engines will leave some of the engine in view, due to the smallish size of the cowling, although slanting such an engine may conceal it better than a straight, inverted mounting. Cowling and wheel pants are available; ordering details on the plan.

Gear legs are made from 1/4 and 7/32 inch piano wire. Full sized patterns appear on the plan. These are both simple shapes and will be readily bent to shape with a suitable bender.

Tail members are all 3/8 inch sheet stock and rib locations are shown. Ribs may be simulated with 1/8 inch square balsa stock, if desired.

Wing construction is usual model practice. Wing panels are built separately and, since only one panel is shown on the plan, one must be built on the back of the plan sheet. The wing center section is built as part of the fuselage and two maple spars project from it onto which the wing slides for flight.

The wing panels are constant chord so only a minimum of wing ribs must be patterned and cut. All ribs are cap-stripped after assembly. Separate aileron servos are shown at mid-point of the aileron in each wing. This location will require rather long servo leads to reach the receiver, so here again, check that the radio suffers no interference from the extra length of wire involved. (Ace Noise Traps should be used if there is any doubt about the ability of the radio to reject such signals.)

The wing struts are functional and necessary for flight, of course. They should be constructed with care, assuring that all mounting hardware and connections are solid and flight-worthy. The fuselage end of the strut mount is silver soldered together. It should be noted that this is not ordinary solder. This joint must bear the flight loads of holding the wings in place and must be made up securely.

With a wing loading of 24 ounces per square foot, the Vagabond will be an excellent flyer. This is providing it's weight is held close to that specified. It could be a good deal heavier and still fly well. While nothing out of the ordinary so far as it's appearance is concerned, the Vagabond should have no bad habits and be an easy model to fly. It should be kept in mind that such airplanes are not fully aerobatic in full scale, so the model should be flown accordingly.

DEGREE OF DIFFICULTY:

While there is a good deal of construction here, as there is in most large models, there is nothing to give trouble to the experienced builder. The newcomer could also build the Vagabond with some help from an experienced model builder. Our '3' so indicates. Good flying, good looking, and very stable.

1/3rd SCALE

POBER PIXIE

FROM: Ken Runestrand, 301 Bitner St., Roseville, Ca. 95678

SPAN: 120" **CHORD: 18"** **DOD: 3** **AREA: 2100 Sq.In.**

LENGTH: 72" **WEIGHT: 24#** **ENGINE: Quadra 35**

HISTORICAL:

Paul Poberenzy, who practically single-handedly founded the Experimental Aircraft Association (EAA), began designing and building the first Pober Pixie in January, 1974. The first flight of the airplane took place in July of that same year and it appeared at the EAA Fly-In at Oshkosh, Wisconsin in August. Surely, it was some sort of record for the conception, design and construction of an airplane.

The Pixie was, if anything, a reincarnation of the Heath Parasol of 1927 with a larger fuselage, more modern materials and powered by a converted Volkswagen engine. Considering its low empty weight of only 720 pounds and its 98 square feet of wing area, the Pixie is close to being a powered glider. It has docile and forgiving flying characteristics.

Over 900 sets of plans have been sold for the Pixie. The plan set consists of fifteen

18x23" sheets. Cost of building the Pixie is estimated to be between $5,000 and $7,000. Construction will require between 1,200 and 1,500 hours. Since there are now pre-fabbed parts available, the Pixie is truly a "do-it-yourself" airplane. The fuselage is welded steel tubing as are the tail feathers. The wings are wood framed and the entire airplane is fabric covered. While most VW engine conversions can be used, some models have been powered with the flat four SL 1700 Limbach engine of 60 HP.

PLAN:

The three model plan sheets are about as stark and un-adorned as you'll find. But this is a very simple airplane and one that doesn't require a lot of detail. What isn't needed, hasn't been added. There is enough detail present to build this good looking model and that's what counts. (Note: see Scale R/C Modeler October 1984 for the write up on the model by the designer.)

The Pixie is something quite different and has some considerable aerobatic potential as well. The engine used in the prototype was a Q35 and this will provide more than adequate power for this model. Cowl, wheel pants and landing gear are available from T & D Fiberglass Specialties.

Fuselage construction makes use of plywood side panels (Lite-Ply or Mahogany door-skin). No stiffening is shown inside the plywood sides with the exception of the firewall and three interior formers. Nothing further should be required. Upper and lower fuselage formers are quite simple in shape and will be no problem to pattern and cut.

Landing gear is 3/16 inch wire and, while silver soldering is recommended, the use of the high heat required to silver solder will likely draw the temper from the wire making it rather soft. It must be re-tempered after being assembled. A better idea is the use of so-called 'baling' wire and a slightly higher temperature soft solder.

Tail group parts are made from stick stock. Shapes are quite simple and should present no problems. Some small metal parts will be required, such as steering arms which connect the rudder to the CB Associates tail wheel. Hinges recommended are also CB Associates and the method of mounting them requires the lamination of the hinged members. A screw is then used to retain the hinges in place. This permits removal of the surfaces if it's ever required.

Both wing panels are shown and, as the wing is constant chord, it requires a minimum of wing rib patterns and parts cutting. Ailerons are almost full span and a doubled aileron linkage is used to assure they are moved as required by control inputs. Separate servos are used in each wing panel; required with such large ailerons. Ribs are all cap-stripped so a good deal of time will be spent here, cutting and assembling them all.

CB Associates strap hinges are shown on the ailerons and a trimmed piece of 1 inch quarter round is shown as the aileron leading edge. If this is a problem, a conventional alternate is shown as well. The airfoil used is flat bottomed, so the wing assembly will be easily accomplished on a flat building surface.

The wings attach to the semi-permanently mounted center section through the use of concentric aluminium tubing. The method of holding the wings in place is not shown on the plan, but pictures of the model show four bolt or screw heads on top of the center section, so it is safe to assume these pass through both pieces of the concentric tubing, making a solid connection.

The wing struts are functional so they must be made and attached properly in order to withstand the flight loads imposed.

Cabane struts require some silver soldering and here again, care should be taken not to draw the temper of the wire although it is less important here than in the landing gear. The assembly of the cabane struts is a little out of the ordinary but is shown in detail on the plan. The cabane strut assembly is a very strong one and well designed.

DEGREE OF DIFFICULTY:

Our rating of '3' leans slightly in the direction of a '2'. Anyone with a few kits or a plan or two behind them should have no difficulty with this good looking, fine flying, model.

1/4 SCALE (28%)

STARDUSTER TOO

FROM: U.S. Quadra, 1032 East Manitowoc Ave., Oak Creek, Wisconsin. 53154

SPAN: 82" (U) 72 3/4" (L) CHORD: 13 (Max.) AREA: 1420 Sq. In. (Approx.)

LENGTH: 64 1/2" WEIGHT: Unspecified DOD: 4 ENGINE: Q35

HISTORICAL:

'Elegant' is the word to describe the Starduster Too! A home-built design of the Stolp Starduster Corp., the twin/tandem seat biplane is a stunner. Developed from the single-seat Stolp SA-100, the Too can be powered by engines from 125 HP to 260 (the latter providing true aerobatic performance.

Size-wise, the Starduster Too is a relatively small aircraft. The upper wing spans a mere 24 feet and the fuselage is 20' long. Wing area is a respectable 162 sq. ft. Max. Gross weight approximates 1800 lbs. The beautiful elliptical wings are "the" identification feature of the Starduster series of aircraft.

Plans for the full-size craft are relatively inexpensive and the designer has provided information (useful for documentation purposes) at a reasonable figure. It shouldn't be too difficult a chore to locate a 'Too for photographic purposes and the various photo services should have representative photo packets if the modeler doesn't include photography among his hobbies.

PLAN:

This plan for the Starduster Too from US Quadra can only be termed elegant. Dario Brisighella's plans are often so, and this one is no exception. When his plans are first unrolled, most model builders will spend a considerable time admiring the workmanship and detail provided.

The four sheets for the Starduster Too include all of the detail necessary to produce an excellent model from them. As these plans were worked up from a set for the full scale airplane, the Starduster is a fine candidate for the scale builder. Little, if any, deviation from full scale is to be found. A cowl and wheel pants can be purchased from T & D Fiberglass Specialties.

In such detailed plans, it's easy for some detail or other to get 'lost'. In order to prevent such accidental oversights, Brisighella's plans have the fuselage framing members laid out as shaded areas, making them quite obvious to the eye.

Fuselage construction is 'stick', using 3/8 inch square spruce main longerons, top and bottom, along with 1/4 by 3/8 inch balsa diagonal members. Most fuselage joints are gussetted. Framing the bare fuselage will be a simple task for any builder. The main longerons must be notched accurately to accept the tail post before assembly.

The landing gear is made from drive rod material and mild steel rod. A jig for its accurate assembly is shown in detail on the plan. This gear is provided with a spring loaded shock absorbing mechanism and the two halves of the gear are almost separate assemblies. The completed assembly is then faired with balsa for appearance.

The tail group is 'stick' construction with the rudder and elevator sanded to a decreasing cross section at the trailing edge. The elevator is made in separate halves, each half being operated independently by a servo. This is a good practice and will provide some control should one servo fail in the neutral position.

Wing construction is somewhat out of the ordinary, compared to the usual wing. The differences will require some care in cutting wing ribs due to the need for accurate 1/16 inch slots at the trailing edges of both upper and lower wings. Due to the rather elegant elliptical shape of the wings in plan view, every wing rib is different; so, a large number of patterns will be required.

As is common with biplanes, the upper wing is built flat and the lower has a moderate amount of dihedral. The upper wing may be built in one piece or each panel built separately and then joined. If the latter construction technique is chosen, the plan recommends the addition of fiberglass cloth around the joint. This same treatment is advised for the lower wing as well.

Four wing spars, 5/16 inch square spruce, are shown in both the upper and lower wings. The plan suggests these may be changed to balsa if desired, but if this is done, the spars should be webbed.

Two aileron servos are shown and this is excellent practice for a large biplane. Such servos must provide adequate power to move four ailerons, so should be selected with care. Servos are mounted at the center of the wing, a more-or-less conventional pushrod and bellcrank arrangement is used to transmit the movement of the servo arm to the aileron.

Static balance weights are shown added to the ailerons. Details for making these parts is shown, and a construction procedure is recommended. A considerable number of metal parts will be required during construction, so metal working experience (and tools) are a necessity.

DEGREE OF DIFFICULTY:

While not an overly difficult plan, this 'Duster by Dario will require a lot of painstaking work to create what could be an outstanding model. Not for the low time builder. The 'scale addict' will love it. Our '4' indicates that this one should not be taken on by anyone but the dedicated and accomplished builder.

CHALLENGER (SPORT MODEL)

FROM: BILL TRUE, 3105 Sudbury Lane, Louisville, Kentucky. 40220

SPAN: 72 1/2" (U) 68 1/4" (L) CHORD: 10 3/4" AREA: 1513 Sq. In.

LENGTH: 60 3/4" WEIGHT: Not Specified DOD: I ENGINE: QUADRA 35

HISTORICAL:

As this is a "sport" biplane model, no full sized airplane exists. Bill True designed the Challenger as a large model, easily built and with good flying characteristics. The wing area, control surface areas and moment arms are generous and should provide a model which will fly well, providing quite gentle handling characteristics, but capable of at least moderate aerobatics with the throttle advanced.

PLAN:

The plan for the Challenger is not the thorough, copiously referenced drawing of a Brisighella, but is adequate to build the model. It's a little rough-hewn in spots and some of the material called out (especially in the horizontal stabilizer and elevator, rudder and fin) is substantially larger than is necessary. Somewhat lighter material could be used without compromising strength to any degree at all.

The fuselage sides are made of Lite-Ply braced with an internal stick structure. This will provide more than adequate strength and the structure should be able to withstand more than the usual amount of abuse without failing.

The landing gear mounts to a 1/4" plywood plate which also serves as a hatch, presumably for access to the fuel compartment, although this is not specified.

The cabane struts are 1/4" plywood and the interplane struts are made up from 1/8" ply. These are much stronger than is necessary and somewhat smaller parts (and/or lighter material) could be used.

No radio location or control hook-up is shown, so the rank beginner should plan to get some help when it comes time to install the radio equipment. It would be well to discuss this with an experienced modeler prior to starting construction, in order to avoid problems after construction has progressed too far.

The wings are one piece, which is not a problem except with a very small car. Spars are called out as 'hardwood' but it is presumed one of the softwoods, such as spruce, is intended. Front spars are 1/4 X 3/8 inch and the rear upper spar is 1/4 square and the lower is 1/4 X 1/8 inches. Only the lower wing has any dihedral, the upper wing is flat.

The airfoil used is not specified, but is semi-symmetrical, which should result in an aerobatic capability for the model,particularly with the power specified. The upper wing is swept a few degrees which makes for slightly more difficult construction, but nothing to cause great concern.

DEGREE OF DIFFICULTY:

The Challenger is quite a simple model and should create no difficulty for anyone who has built a kit or two. Even the rank newcomer should not have any real difficulty with it so long as he is able to transfer patterns, and cut accurately shaped parts from them. The absolute beginner should either try to get some advice from an experienced model builder on those matters not covered by the plan, or should read the very good Flight Training Course, Volume I, put out by R C Modeler Magazine. Alternatively, the book, "Building Big Is Beautiful" by one of the authors is another good source of material on the construction of large models.

COMMENTS:

The Challenger is not a particularly pretty model. It is structurally quite sound, and, as mentioned above, should be able to absorb a good deal of normal day-to-day abuse without damage. As the weight is un-specified, it is rather difficult to estimate the wing loading, and therefore flying traits it will show. However, there is a great deal of wing area and even if the model came out at 25 pounds (which is unlikely) wing loading would be 38 oz/sq. ft. Getting up there, but still flyable. It should be kept at or under 20 pounds if at all possible and will be an excellent sport model at that weight.

LARGE FLOATS
(22 TO 32 POUND MODEL)

FROM: Wendell Hostetler, 1041 Heatherwood Lane, Orrville, Ohio. 44667

PLAN:

Specifications and sizes of a set of floats would not have much meaning. These are claimed to be able to support models in the range of 22 to 32 pounds weight, and, other than that, there isn't a lot to say.

The plan is Hostetler's usual clear and uncluttered work. The patterns for the floats are shown as are those for the mounting wires to the airplane. The building instructions are right on the plan, all 24 steps, so there should be no problem with making them.

A water rudder is shown and should be installed. Water borne airplanes are difficult to control in a wind; without water rudder(s), they are impossible. A method of permitting the rudder to swing up (retract) is shown and this can be modified to provide spring tension to the lowered position. A small plate attached to the rudder at right angles to the direction of travel will cause the rudder to swing up, out of the way at speeds above which it is not required.

Both floats may require rudders installed and a connecting 'tiller-bar' used to tie them together. One rudder of adequate size is usually enough to provide good steering. The water rudder may be operated directly from the air rudder, indirectly from the rudder servo, or from a servo operating from a 'Y' harness in conjunction with the air rudder.

Be sure to use a waterproof glue in assembly. Water will inevitably get inside a float and a water soluble glue may cause your floats to come apart at an inopportune time. A light, thin coating of glass resin inside the floats will add to their longevity. Just be careful not to add too much weight. A very light cloth and resin outside (at least on the bottoms) will provide both strength and an excellent surface on which to finish.

DEGREE OF DIFFICULTY:

A '2' in anybody's league!

1/4 OR 1/3 SCALE EDO FLOATS

FROM: Ken Runestrand, 301 Bitner St., Roseville, California. 95678

PLAN:

The joys of flying a large model from floats are ones which, once experienced, will not easily be forgotten. The almost unlimited space available from a body of water, and the ability to accommodate almost any wind present, are both welcome improvements over flying from land.

Ken Runestrand has done a nice job in providing a set of floats which will do very well for either 1/4 or 1/3 scale models. This dual purpose is accomplished by adding one former in the larger of the floats, and is quite easily done.

These floats closely resemble the well known Edo float and some additional scale detail is shown which will dress them up to look quite realistic.

Construction is very straight-forward and should not prove difficult for the experienced. As the floats must be assembled away from the plan, care will be required in order to produce a warp free and properly aligned structure. Choosing straight grained stick material will certainly help.

Floats require at least one water rudder to maintain control of a model in even the lightest breezes. Ken's plans show the rudder and it's servo in more than adequate detail for ease of construction. The servo is mounted inside one float and connected to the receiver rudder output, through a 'Y' connector. A sub-fin for the model's fuselage is also shown.

DEGREE OF DIFFICULTY:

Simple construction and easy-to-duplicate shapes will provide even the low time builder with a set of more than adequate floats. A '2' rating for these Edo type floats by Ken Runestrand.

DOCUMENTATION

Although most of us involved in Giant Scale **aren't** primarily interested in competition, we **are** interested in producing models that really look like their prototypes. A Big Bird fly-in is, essentially, a low-pressure get-together of people who like to build, fly, talk-about or just plain, watch large sized radio control models fly. Nine builders/flyers out of ten might never assemble a "documentation book", a necessary element in AMA/International competition.

The following documentation sources have been researched in the preparation of this book. They are in no way, exhaustive. Rather, they represent only a beginning point for any plans builder who wishes to assure the accuracy of the scale model airplane he or she builds from the drawings discussed in this book. Our references range from articles in old model airplane magazines to books that tell the whole story about a particular prototype. These books and magazines may not be readily available to everyone, although most will be in big-city libraries, or from book dealers and purveyors of back-issues. It is important to note that the authors **are not in the documentation business**! You **will find** the names of companies and people who **are,** in the "Sources" section that follows.

A prime source of documentation information is to be found among our brethern who indulge in the hobby of building plastic models. Plastic model kits invariably include color and markings data on their instructions sheets. The models themselves, when built, provide a three-dimensional "look" at how a Giant Scale model will appear in finished form. In order to make the molds for even the most prosiac of plastic models, the manufacturer must thoroughly research the subject of the kit. In fact, the readily-available documentation in plastic kits is one of the largest untapped sources for the average R/C scale model builder. Given this situation, wherever there is (or has been) a plastic kit for a particular model in our Table of Contents, we will note it below.

Finally, we will note the existence of good three-views for the models in our Table of Contents. Here we are being rather subjective, once more. Often there are several three-views for a single subject. Our choice may not be the absolutely best available -- but, they'll usually come close.

Our listing below follows the pattern established by our Table of Contents.

WORLD WAR I

FOKKER EINDECKER (E.III): Aircraft in Profile #38; Neito drawings in MAN's Scale Book #1 (also available in 3/4"=1 ft. from NASM). Aurora offered a plastic kit of the Fokker Eindecker, but it's an expensive collectors' item, today.

FOKKER D.VII: Aircraft in Profile, #25; MAN's Scale Book #1; Neito's definitive drawings are also available, at 3/4"=1 ft., from NASM. Extensive coverage on the D.7 is also available in Cross & Cockade Journals. See D-VII entry for C&C Journal source. Monogram offers a 1/4"=1 ft. plastic model of the D.VII, but it might be hard to find. It's a skilfully reworked Aurora kit, that is a collectors' item.

FOKKER D.VIII: Aircraft in Profile #67. The only really good drawings for the D.8 are to be found in Leo Opdycke's World War I Aero. Check with him for the appropriate issues. Markings information is noted in C&C Journals (see availability information above).

FOKKER TRIPLANE: Aircraft in Profile #55; great Nieto drawings (MAN's Scale Book #1 and NASM); C&C Journals (see availability information above). Revell has a magnificently detailed plastic model of the 'Tripe (Dr.1) in 1/27th scale. It's worth searching for!

FOKKER TRIPLANE, Dr.1: See preceding entry.

SOPWITH "PUP": Aircraft in Profile #13; "Sopwith, The Man and His Aircraft", Robertson, Harleyford Publications.

BETWEEN THE WARS, MILITARY & CIVILIAN A/C

BEECHCRAFT STAGGERWING: "Model Airplane News Presents the Best of Wylam, Book 1" -- for good three-views of **all** the Staggerwing variants; "Staggerwing", by Robert T. Smith, Haney publisher (recently republished and updated!). Beech Acft. Corp. drawing #340744.

BOEING F4B-1/4: Aircraft in Profile #27 (#2, for Boeing P-12E); "U.S. Naval Fighters", by Jones, Aero Publishers; "American Combat Aircraft", by Ray Wagner, published by Hanover House. Particularly exact plastic model available, by Hasegawa (1/32nd scale). Aero Series Volume #5 by Maloney.

BUCKER "JUNGMANN": Aircraft in Profile #222; three-views, Aeromodeller magazine, February, 1974 issue (Aeromodeller drawings are usually available from Bob Holman).

BUCKER "JUNGMEISTER": Aeromodeller had three-view in their October 1958 issue; MAN had three-views in their November, 1958 issue; good data on the Jungmeister is contained in "Die Deutsches Flugzeuge" by Kens & Nowaraa, Lehmann Verlag (in German); "Antique Aircraft", by Chris Sorenson pictures a surviving, stock Jungmeister in Texas.

BUCKER "JUNGMEISTER": See preceding entry.

CURTISS P-6E: "The Curtiss Hawks", by Shamburger & Christy, Wolverine Press; "The Best of Wylam", published by MAN (good three-views); and, there is a restored P-6E at the Air Force Museum, Wright-Patterson AFB, Ohio. Plastic model: 1/72nd scale by Monogram.

FAIRCHILD 22: Good three-views for the '22 that Florence presents in his drawings may be found in the July, 1968 issue of American (Aircraft) Modeller; data may be obtained in Volume 6 of Joe Juptner's "U.S. Civil Aircraft".

GYPSY MOTH: "British Civil Aircraft", by Jackson and published by Putnam; three-views -- May, 1969 issue of American (Aircraft) Modeler.

J-3 "CUB": Volume XVIII of the Historical Aviation Album has great J-3 three-views plus an extensive article on the history of Taylor/Piper aircraft.

J-3 "CUB": See preceeding entry.

KINNER "SPORTSTER": Why knock yourself out when DGA Design has three-views and a photo-pac covering the subject of their drawing? "Yesterday's Wings" by Pete Bowers, AOPA publishers, will give you some excellent background on the subject of Kinner monoplanes.

MONOCOUPE 110-SPL., CLIPPED-WING: "Of Monocoupes and Men, by John Underwood, Caler; "The Golden Age of Air Racing" by Schmid & Weaver, EAA publishers.

PIETENPOL "SKY SCOUT": The **best** reference to the "Sky Scout" is the obscure, 1933 "Modern Mechanix Flying Manual" which includes detailed drawings and data for the "real airplane". The model magazines have published drawings of the "Air Camper" but not the 'Scout. Air Trails published an interesting article on the 'Pete by Pete Bowers in "Sport Aircraft", Winter, 1971. This is a relatively difficult aircraft to document because of its age and the fact that it was a pre-EAA homebuilt. Locating a surviving example and photographing it (or, acquiring a photo-pak from one of the documentation services) is probably the way to go.

RYAN "SPIRIT OF ST. LOUIS": Jim Triggs' three-views (published in the June, 1957 issue of American Aircraft Modeler) are probably the definitive ones. They've been reprinted innumerable times (lately in Scale R/C Modeler). The original is in the NASM and replicas can be found in the EAA Museum and the San Diego Aerospace Museum. If you can't find good documentation information on Lindbergh's NYP, you just ain't trying!

TAYLORCRAFT, CLIPPED-WING: This is a particularly difficult model to document. Our only reference was found in Air Trails' "Sport Aircraft", Winter, 1971 issue.

WACO ARE: Model Builder magazine published good three-views of the Waco SRE in their November, 1973 issue. There are only subtle differences between it and the ARE version (different engine). Good data and photographs for this model may be found in Ray Brandly's "The Versatile Waco Series" and his "Waco Aircraft Production" (self-published, but usually available through Historic Aviation, Eagan, Minnesota).

WACO CTO: Note the Brandly book references in the entry, above.

WACO HKS-7: Brandly references also apply to this entry. Paul Matt has done a beautiful three-view of the YKS-7 that represents, essentially, the same airframe configuration (available from Historic Aviation Album), along with a companion article.

WATERMAN "AEROBILE": Paul Matt did a magnificent documentation job on the Waterman Aerobile in Volume III of the Historic Aviation Album. Although the book itself may be difficult to locate (and expensive to purchase second-hand!), Paul's drawings are still available.

"GOLDEN AGE" RACING AIRPLANES

GEE BEE R-1: "The Golden Age of Air Racing", by Schmid & Weaver, EAA Pub.; Williams Bros. 1/32nd scale plastic kit -- which also includes good three-views by Bill Hannan as well as decals that contain all of the markings.

"GILMORE" (WEDELL-WILLIAMS RACER): The "Golden Age" book noted above is a prime reference; the Williams Bros. also produce an excellent 1/32nd scale Wedell-Williams Racer plastic kit whose decals and painting instructions show how to make three different versions -- you can use the info to modify Hostetler's drawings (!); the American Air Racing Society (see "Source" section for the address) publishes a number of particularly excellent Kerka drawings for the Wedell-Williams Racer, at 3/4"=1 ft.

HAWK'S "TIME FLYS": "The Golden Age of Air Racing" by Schmid & Weaver, EAA Pub.

TURNER-LAIRD LTR-14: Paul Matt's Historical Aviation Album, Volume 10, contains practically everything you'll need to document the LTR-4, including excellent three-views! Larger-scale drawings are still available from Paul.

WORLD WAR II "WARBIRDS"

CURTISS P-40D: "The Curtiss Hawks", by Schaumberger & Christy, Wolverine Press; "U.S. Fighters" by Lloyd Jones, Aero Publishers (includes drawings); "The Best of Wylam", MAN pub.; Aircraft in Profile #35.

DOUGLAS "SKYRAIDER": "American Combat Aircraft" by Ray Wagner, Hanover House; Aircraft in Profile #60.

FAIRCHILD PT-19: MAN, March 1969 issue (three-views); Paul Matt drawings #AA-69-A.

FLEET "FINCH": "Ruben Fleet, and the Story of the Consolidated Aircraft Co., by Ray Wagner, Aero Publishers; MAN, March 1943 issue (three-views) -- this is a relatively difficult aircraft to document due to the proliferation of Fleet biplane designs.

GRUMMAN "BEARCAT" F8F: "U.S. Navy Fighters", by Lloyd Jones, Aero Publishers (includes drawings of stock F8F); good Monogram plastic kit.

NORTH AMERICAN AT-6 (HARVARD): Paul Matt's Historical Aviation Album, Volume #16 has most of what you'll need, including good three-views and an article written by one of the authors of this book(!); Monogram offers a good (plastic) "Texan" in 1/48th scale.

RYAN XPT-16: "Ryan Guidebook", by Carpenter & Mayborn, American Aircraft Series, Book 3; three-views may be found in the January, 1941 issue of MAN -- if you can find a copy. Happily, a PT-16 survives in California and the photo-documentation people have good colored pictures of it available.

STEARMAN PT-13 (NAVY N2S): Stearman Guidebook by Mayborn & Bowers, Flying Enterprises Publications; good three-view in the October, 1961 issue of American (Aircraft) Modeler -- of the PT-13(!); Lindberg still offers a Stearman plastic kit in 1/48th scale.

VOUGHT "CORSAIR" (F4U-1): "Aeroplanes Vought", by Gerard P. Moran, Historical Aviation Album pub; Paul Matt drawings, #AA-51-A; Aircraft in Profile #'s 47 & 150; both Monogram and Revell make good F4U plastic kits.

VOUGHT "KINGFISHER" (OS2-U): "Aeroplanes Vought", as referenced above; three-views may be found in MAN, March 1972 issue; Monogram offered a great 1/48th scale Kingfisher plastic kit, which may be difficult to find, but worth the search.

WESTLAND "LYSANDER": MAN offers Wylam's great 4-page set of drawings and they may also be found in "The Best of Wylam" from the same source; Matchbox produces their 1/32nd scale plastic kit (#PK 504) for the Lysander that's almost "jewel-like", and has good color documentation as well.

POST-WAR CIVILIAN A/C & HOMEBUILTS

DRUINE "TURBULENT": Flying Models, July, 1956 issue, has good three-views; "Sport Aircraft", Winter 1971 issue has specs.

ERCOUPE: "Yesterday's Wings" by Pete Bowers, AOPA; the "latest" magazine three-view reference to the Ercoupe (Aircoupe, et al) was in the July, 1950 issue of the Aeromodeler -- which doesn't help a whole bunch! Happily, the photo-pak people have pictures.

GRUMMAN "AGCAT": Scale Model Research (Bob Banka -- see "Source" section) has a great photo-pak on the AGCAT. Finding three-views is another kettle of fish! They're "out there", but we can't uncover 'em.

PIPER "SKYCYCLE": MAN, November, 1945 has Wylam three-views as does American Modeler in their January, 1960 issue; there's good reference material on the craft in the June, 1969 issue of Sport Flying. Wylam drawings reprinted in "The Best of Wylam", MAN.

PIPER "VAGABOND": Volume 9 of Joe Juptner's "U.S. Civil Aircraft" is the best reference to the PA-17 "Vagabond".

POBER "PIXIE": We found the specs. for the Pixie in "Sport Aircraft", Winter 1971 issue; and drawings are available from the EAA.

STARDUSTER "TOO": Dario's drawings are so precise that it seems redundant to have to document his outlines and color schemes. We found specs. in the "Sport Aircraft" magazine referenced above and the photo-documentation people have stunning Starduster photo-paks. An info-pack has been available for a nominal charge from the Starduster people.

DOCUMENTATION NOTES

You will note that some of the references indicated above are rather obscure. For most of us, magazines from the 40's, 50's and 60's are difficult to come-by. A dedicated scale modeler may be inclined to thrash with people who sell back-issue magazines in order to have an "original" three-view at hand. However, there are two sources of this sort of documentation that are much, much easier to "tap". 'Doc Pepino (Scale Plans and Photo Service, 3209 Madison Ave., Greensboro, North Carolina, 27403) offers a "search service" through his extensive collection of three-views for a very nominal fee. Dick Gleason (1106 10th Drive, S.E., Austin, Minnesota, 55912) offers a similar service.

Several of our documentation entries indicate reference to "Aircraft in Profile", usually referred to as "Profiles". For an extended period of time, Profiles were out of print. They are, currently, being reprinted on a selective basis (mostly for the WW II "Warbirds") and are being offered by Zenith Aviation. We do wish to caution anyone using Profiles as color reference that they not try to "match" the printed colors. Like any color printing, Profiles are limited in their ability to produce precise hues. We recommend, particularly for military aircraft, that scale model builders refer directly to available color chips for proper colors.

Finally, one of the "untapped" documentation sources for R/C scale models is the designer, himself! Certainly, he had to have data, photographs and three-views in order to prepare the drawings. Don't expect the designer to prepare your documentation booklet -- and, count yourself lucky if he responds with a list of references. If you go this "route", be sure to include a stamped, self-addressed envelope (business size).

SOURCES

The following "sources" can provide anything from a photo-pak to a complete kit for some of the models described in this book. There are addresses for people who supply fiberglass parts for some of the models described in this book. We have, also, included, the names and addresses of companies and individuals whose business it is to manufacture those necessary accessory items. Most of the "sources" are model builders, themselves, who have "branched out". They understand our problems and are willing to help those of us who need their services. However, since we're talking "small business", please be patient when you write or phone them -- and include a stamped, self-addressed envelope. Postage is a big nick out of their bank accounts and the SASE will, certainly, be appreciated.

NATIONAL AIR & SPACE MUSEUM (SMITHSONIAN INSTITUTION): Fiscal Division, Section M, Smithsonian Institution, Washington, D.C., 20560 (Neito drawings)

NASM, Aircraft Drawings 80-952, 3904 Old Silver Hill Rd., Suitland, MD, 20023 (for drawing other than Neito's)

U.S. AIR FORCE MUSEUM, Wright-Patterson AFB, Dayton, OH, 45433

NATIONAL AERONAUTICAL COLLECTION (CANADA), Hangar 68, CFB Ottowa North, Ontario, Canada

AMERICAN AVIATION HISTORICAL SOCIETY, P.O. Box 99, Garden Grove, CA, 92642 (quarterly journals that include photos and drawings)

CANADIAN MUSEUM OF FLIGHT & TRANSPORTATION, 11040 Cambie Road, Richmond, B.C., Canada, V6X 1L2

THE BOEING CO., HISTORICAL SERVICES DIVISION, P.O. 3707, Mail Stop 11-24, Seattle, WA, 98124

C.G. ENTERPRISES, P.P. Box 651, Hesperia, CA, 92345 (good B&W photos)

BOB HOLMAN PLANS, P.O. Box 741, San Bernardino, CA, 92402 (Aeromodeller drawings)

MORRISON REPLA-TECH INTERNATIONAL, 48500 McKenzie Hwy., Vida, OR, 97488 (photos and drawings)

SCALE AEROTECH, 21028 Golden Triangle Rd., Saugus, CA, 91350 (drawings)

RARE BIRDS, 791 Nisqually Dr., Sunnyvale, CA, 94087

SCALE PLANS & PHOTO SERVICE, 3209 Madison Ave., Greensboro, NC, 27403 (see Documentation Notes)

DICK GLEASON, 1106 10th Drive, S.E., Austin, MN, 55912

SCALE MODEL RESEARCH, 2334 Ticonderoga Way, Costa Mesa, CA, 92626 (photos and drawings -- Bob Banka

MODEL AIRPLANE NEWS (MAN), 837 Post Road, Darien, CT, 06820 (drawings, books of three-views)

MODEL AVIATION, (MA) 1810 Samuel Morse Dr., Reston, VA, 22090

MODEL BUILDER, 898 W. 16th St., Newport Beach, CA, 92663

SCALE R/C MODELER, c/o Challenge Publications, 7950 Deering Ave., Canoga Park, CA, 91304

RADIO CONTROL MODELER, P.O. Box 487, Sierra Madre, CA, 91024

FLYING MODELS, P.O. Box 700, Newton, NJ, 07860

HISTORIC AVIATION, 3850 Coronation Rd., Eagan, MN, 55122 (books)

ZENITH AVIATION BOOKS, c/o Motorbooks International, 729 Prospect Ave., Osceola, WI, 54020

C.B. ASSOCIATES, 21658 Cloud Way, Hayward, CA, 94545

ACE R/C, P.O. Box 511, Higginsville, MO, 64037

AMERICAN AIR RACING SOCIETY, c/o Rudy Profant, 4060 W. 158th St., Cleveland, OH, 44135 (great Kerka drawings of Golden Age racing aircraft)

U.S. QUADRA, 1032 E. Manitowoc Ave., Oak Creek, WI, 53154

KIT COLLECTORS' CLEARING HOUSE (John Burns), 3213 Hardy Dr., Edmond, OK, 73034 (publishes listings of out-of-production plastic models!)

CASTLE GRAPHICS, P.O. Box AD, Greenbank, WA, 98253 (source of photos from Pete Bowers' collection)

COLLECT-AIR PHOTOS, P.O. Box 14234, Milwaukee, WI, 53214

CROSS & COCKADE, GT. BRITAIN, (Mrs. Christine A. Leaman, Membership Secretary), Cragg Cottage, The Cragg, Bramham Wetherby, West Yorkshire, LS 23 6QB, England

CROSS & COCKADE, U.S. (back-issues only!), Harry Miller, P.O. Box U, Norwalk, CA, 90651

DU BRO PRODUCTS, 480 Bonner Rd., Wauconda, IL, 60084

EAA, P.O. Box 229, Hales Corners, WI, 53130

HISTORICAL AVIATION ALBUM (Paul Matt), Available from: SunShine House, Inc., P.O. Box 2065, Terre Haute, IN, 47802.

NATIONAL ASSOCIATION OF SCALE AEROMODELLERS, (Bert Dugan, Secretary/Treasurer) 11090 Phyllis Dr., Clio, MI, 48420

WORLD WAR I AEROPLANES (Leo E. Opdycke) 15 Crescent Rd., Poughkeepsie, NY, 12601 (WW I & Golden Age magazines -- with good documentation drawings and photos)

LEAGUE OF WORLD WAR I AVIATION HISTORIANS, (James L. Kerr, Treasurer) P.O. Box 780265, Dallas, TX, 75378-0265 (publish "Over the Front", successor to C&C, U.S.)

JOHN POND OLD TIME PLAN SERVICE, P.O. Box 90310, San Jose, CA, 95109-3310

ROYAL PRODUCTS, 790 W. Tennessee Ave., Denver, CO, 80223

SAN DIEGO AEROSPACE MUSEUM, 2001 Pan American Plaza, Balboa Park, San Diego, CA, 92101

SCALE DOCUMENTATION

The scale modeler is continually faced with the task of documenting the accuracy of his model when compared to the original airplane. In most cases, we don't have the opportunity to inspect the 1:1 original we wish to model, so must make use of photographs to provide us with the detailed information we need.

To be of use to us, the photos used must provide as much detail of the original airplane as possible; they must be readily available for a wide variety of aircraft; they should be color photos; there should be a good assortment of views, and they should be reasonably priced.

Now that's a pretty tall order if you think about it for a minute. While it's true each of us who build scale models might require perhaps 50 different sets of documentation photos during a modeling career, multiply that by the number who require them and you could come up with a very large number indeed.

Which is exactly what Bob Banka of Scale Model Research has done. He has more than 1800 subjects and a total of over 50,000 photos in stock. That is anything but a static figure. During the summer of 1986, Bob added a significant number of additional airplanes to his stock in trade. For example, during the summer mentioned, Bob visited the USAF Museum at Wright Patterson in Dayton Ohio, the EAA meet at Oshkosh and the Blakesburg, Iowa Antique Fly In. All of which supplied a large number of subjects for Bob's stock. In the Summer of 1987, he added another 300 subjects.

These are more than just pretty pictures. With Bob's knowledge of what the modeler requires, he attempts to take pictures of the detail we need in order to create our aircraft in miniature. Instrument panels, landing gear detail, control surface hinges, paint and trim details, cowl attach points, engine and exhaust systems, in short as much as possible of the internal and external detail required to duplicate the original airplane.

In addition to his large stock of photographs, Bob also stocks the well-known Koku-Fan 3 views from Japan. These are recognized as definitive works and Bob has 3,000 in stock, representing over 500 different subjects. In addition, he has recently added another set of drawings with over 250 subjects. He has plans to add "pilot reports" and "color" reports on aircraft in the near future.

As a source for detail, or as required 3 views for your documentation package, the Koku-Fan drawings are among the very best available. It would be possible to scale them to almost any desired size in order to create your own plan, and they are considered one of the most accurate series of drawings available anywhere.

If you'd like more information, send for Bob's catalogue. Cost is $3.00 for a 40-page copy.

SCALE MODEL RESEARCH

2334 Ticonderoga Way,
Costa Mesa, CA, 92626
(714) 979-8058